INTRODUCTION

TO

ADVOCACY

BRIEFWRITING AND ORAL ARGUMENT
IN MOOT COURT

FIFTH EDITION

Prepared By

**BOARD OF STUDENT ADVISERS
HARVARD LAW SCHOOL
CAMBRIDGE, MASSACHUSETTS**

Westbury, New York
THE FOUNDATION PRESS, INC.
1991

Library of Congress Cataloging-in-Publication Data

Introduction to advocacy : briefwriting and oral argument in moot
  court / prepared by Board of Student Advisers, Harvard
  Law School, Cambridge, Massachusetts. — 5th ed.
        p.   cm.
  Includes index.
  ISBN 0–88277–880–3
  1. Moot courts. 2. Briefs—United States. I. Harvard Law
School. Board of Student Advisers.
KF281.A2I57 1991
808'.066347—dc20   91–9616

Intro. to Advocacy 5th Ed.

∞

PREFACE TO THE FIFTH EDITION

The Fifth Edition of *Introduction to Advocacy* is a stylistically enhanced yet streamlined revision of the fourth edition. We believe that the Fifth Edition has a fresher style that will help law students begin to master all the essential elements of the moot court process—research, writing, citation, and oral advocacy. The Fifth Edition contains a section on the scope of appellate review, a question not addressed in previous editions but often explored by judges in moot court exercises. Also, we have altered the chapter format of the fourth edition a bit, making what was formerly Chapter V "General Rules of Style and Citation of Authorities" an appendix. This was done because *A Uniform System of Citation*, "The Bluebook", published by the Harvard Law Review Association is more useful as an authority on citation form and we feel that it was neither possible nor desirable for us to duplicate their efforts in detailing the numerous rule changes. We have retained this appendix as a source for basic reference, but urge students to consult the Bluebook for more complicated citation questions.

The primary new benefit of the Fifth Edition is the revised and expanded chapter on "Researching the Brief." Working in conjunction with Alan Diefenbach, Senior Reference Librarian at Harvard Law School, the Fifth Edition includes what we feel is a comprehensive guide for law students undertaking legal research. This chapter describes all the materials a first-time brief writer is likely to encounter. It also contains a concise discussion of the basic legal research techniques and provides several illustrations to give students a firm working knowledge of how to find and use various research sources. There is explicit guidance on the use of *Shepard's Citations* as well as a complete list of those standard legal research texts which provide more detailed discussions. While the insights provided in this new chapter will prove valuable to any brief writer, it is especially tailored to first-year students.

*

ACKNOWLEDGEMENT

Introduction to Advocacy originally appeared in pamphlet form to guide first-year students at Harvard Law School through the required moot court program. It metamorphosed into book form twenty-one years ago and has been revised four times since then, but not without significant help.

We would like to thank the following members of the Harvard Law School faculty for their comments on the Fourth Edition and whose suggestions we tried to incorporate in this Fifth Edition: Archibald Cox, Jeffrey Kobrick, Daniel Meltzer, Martha Minow, David Rosenberg, and Kathleen Sullivan. Also, we would like to thank Alan Diefenbach, Senior Reference Librarian at Harvard Law School, for his invaluable contributions of time, energy and ideas in revising the chapter "Researching the Brief."

This book was revised by a subcommittee of the Board of Student Advisers, and the members of that committee deserve tremendous praise. Wendy Bloom, Anthony Brown, Ron Goldstein, David Hill and Doug Rappaport contributed substantial amounts of time and energy to this worthy project.

BOARD OF STUDENT ADVISERS

May 1991

*

SUMMARY OF CONTENTS

*

TABLE OF CONTENTS

TABLE OF CONTENTS

TABLE OF CONTENTS

TABLE OF CONTENTS

INTRODUCTION

TO

ADVOCACY

BRIEFWRITING AND ORAL ARGUMENT IN MOOT COURT

*

Chapter I

INTRODUCTION

First-year students at many law schools participate in a moot court program, an exercise that allows students to develop skills in brief-writing and oral advocacy. The reason for this requirement is simple—learning to be an effective advocate is an essential part of every lawyer's education. Of course, not every lawyer is a litigator, and many never see the inside of a courtroom. But regardless of the area of law practiced, every lawyer would undoubtedly agree that the importance of having good written and oral advocacy skills cannot be overstated.

As a participant in a moot court program, you will find that the process of writing a brief develops your ability to formulate legal theories, write convincing arguments, and research persuasive authorities. The oral advocacy aspect of the program allows you to practice the art of "thinking on your feet." During your oral argument, you will be asked questions and presented with issues about which you may not have previously thought, but nevertheless you will be expected to respond intelligently and persuasively.

The typical model for a moot court program is an appellate case. These are cases which have already been decided by a court, and now the appellant is seeking a review of the decision by a higher judicial authority. Your task will be to analyze the history and facts of the case, the decision reached in the court below and the rationale for that decision.

To help you in that task this book has three interrelated goals: 1) to describe how to accomplish every stage of a moot court exercise; 2) to illustrate the narrative descriptions with specific examples; and 3) to serve as a resource that you can refer to at any point during the program.

The structure of the book reflects these goals. Each chapter that follows covers a discrete topic: Reading the Record; Researching the Brief; Writing the Brief; Oral Argument; and Citation. Examples and illustrations in every chapter are drawn from *Bell-Wesley v. O'Toole,* a hypothetical "wrongful birth" suit brought by parents of an unplanned child against the doctor who negligently performed the husband's vasectomy. The full moot court record appears at p. 11; sample briefs for both the appellants and the appellee are at p. 62, immediately following the chapter on briefwriting. These briefs reflect ideas and approaches used by many first year students who researched and

1

argued *Bell-Wesley v. O'Toole* in the moot court program at Harvard Law School.

This book is about moot courts, not real courts. Much of what it has to say about briefwriting and oral argument is applicable to appellate litigation in general, but you should be aware that moot court has characteristics that distinguish it from appellate practice in the "real world." For example, moot court judges—frequently law school professors or upperclass students—often scrutinize the briefs prior to argument and are perhaps more likely than an actual judge to quiz an oralist on her knowledge of specific cases. Frequently, moot court judges will discuss your performance with you after the argument in order to point out strengths and offer suggestions on how to improve weaknesses. Real judges often do not have the time to tutor the attorneys who come before them. Many moot court cases are argued in mythical jurisdictions where no precedent controls but all precedents may have persuasive value. Real cases arise in places where particular statutes and case law not only apply but are binding. Finally, in some moot court programs students work in teams of four, with two students representing appellants and two representing appellees. The four team members collaborate on research and preparation throughout the exercise. When it comes time to argue the case, the pairs split up and argue against students on another team. This approach enables each side to see the strengths and weaknesses of its position and learn how an opponent would characterize the same facts from a contrary perspective. This symmetric collaboration does not exist in the "real world."

Despite the differences, there are many similarities. As in real courts, moot court rules set limits on the length of briefs and oral arguments. Moot court participants are constrained by the contents of the hypothetical trial record in the same way that appellate lawyers are constrained by an actual record. Moot court arguments are often heard by a panel of judges, as they are in federal and state appellate courts.

One final and very important similarity between moot court programs and the litigation of an actual case is the need for you to make strategic and stylistic choices concerning your arguments throughout the process. The art of advocacy is just that—an art, and therefore is necessarily a product of your own tastes and personality. This guide in no way purports to present the "definitive" way to approach written and oral advocacy. Rather, it will simply provide a framework for advocacy which must be filled with your own style and your own strategy.

Chapter II

READING THE RECORD

In appellate moot court competition, as in real life appeals, the record is the lawyer's sole source of information about the facts of the case. The record for the appeal compiles all the legal and factual determinations made by the lower court and includes the various pleadings and motions the parties filed in the lower court, as well as the trial transcript, affidavits of various witnesses, and the lower court opinion. In a moot court record the various documents usually appear in an abbreviated form. An actual record can be thousands of pages; the usual moot court record will be much shorter. The sample record in *Bell-Wesley v. O'Toole,* which follows this chapter, is a typical example.

Read the record closely and carefully in order to discover the factual and legal issues presented in the lower court. Your job on appeal is to examine the lower court's decision closely to determine the precise legal grounds for the opinion, the potential issues of reversible error, the standard of review, and the available arguments for your position. Because the record is your only source of factual information, a clear understanding of the record is prerequisite to an effective appeal.

A. THE PROCESS

There is no single way to read and understand the record. Each person needs to determine what method is best for him. One possible approach is as follows:

1. Read the entire record.

2. Sketch a chronology of what happened.

3. Narrow the issues for appeal.

4. Consider the standard of appellate review.

5. Formulate arguments.

6. Connect the facts to the legal issues.

7. Develop a core theory.

8. Consider opposing arguments and core theories.

9. Read the rules.

10. Read through the whole record again and again, until you have a firm grasp of what it contains.

3

1. Read the Entire Record. Before trying to distill and narrow the information available to you in the record, you must have a broad overview of the case. A first read-through, even a fairly quick one, will help you understand what is happening both legally and factually. With a broad overview, you can begin to narrow the legal and factual problems for the appeal.

2. Sketch a Chronology. The items in a record are not necessarily arranged in the order in which events actually happened. By writing out a chronology of events, you will have a comprehensive and detailed understanding of the factual setting. This is important because many cases turn on not what happened but when it happened.

For example, in *Bell-Wesley v. O'Toole,* one of the important issues in determining whether damages should be awarded is whether Frank's birth harmed Rebecca Bell-Wesley's career goals. You need to look at the trial record of Rebecca's testimony to learn about her potential lost career opportunities. A reading of the record shows that Rebecca became pregnant after she accepted a new position at the attorney general's office. This is very important because if Rebecca had become pregnant before she accepted the new position, she would be less likely to successfully claim damages.

In ordering the facts, you will also discover what facts you do not have. In any court record, moot or otherwise, some facts will be missing or ambiguous. Once you notice what facts are missing, look more closely at the record to see if these facts are hidden or if they can be reasonably inferred from available facts. Facts inferred from the record should become a part of your argument and may be introduced in the Statement of Facts. If you choose to include them in the Statement of Facts, be sure to preface them in a way that signals to the court that you are making an inference. Remember that the only undisputed facts are those in the record. Nothing will defeat your credibility with a court more than the misuse of facts or the use of inference as undisputed fact.

As you read the record, be aware of the varying importance that the court attaches to each fact. Typically, the appellate court will give the greatest weight to the findings of fact of the lower court. The extent to which the appellate court defers to the lower court's findings of fact is dependent upon the standard of review that the appellate court adopts for the issue. (See p. 7, Section 4. Consider the Standard of Appellate Review.) In reviewing the findings of fact in a civil case, the appellate court will review the facts of the case as presented in the plaintiff's complaint, in the defendant's answer, and in trial transcripts. The facts presented by the parties and witnesses are less significant than the findings of fact of the trial judge and jury. However, facts that are stipulated by both parties are undisputed and, therefore, are not reviewed by the appellate courts.

3. Narrow the Issues for Appeal. At the lower court level, many issues are decided. In narrowing the issues for appeal, focus on policy, legal, and factual questions raised by the record. On appeal, the legal issues are normally narrower and more defined than at the lower court.

Determine which of the lower court's decisions are at issue on appeal so that you concentrate only on relevant facts and issues. Sometimes the court will limit the issues for you, as on the last page of the *Bell-Wesley v. O'Toole* record. (See p. 25.) After reading this, you know that you need not consider the possible negligence arguments concerning the vasectomy.

Probably the best places to discover and understand the relevant legal and factual issues on appeal are the lower court opinion and questions to be certified. It discusses the reasons for the court's ruling and should frame the issues for appeal. In *Bell-Wesley v. O'Toole*, the judge's fifth and sixth conclusions of law point you to the two vital issues on appeal: can there be damages for a "wrongful birth," and what items should enter into the calculation of these damages. (See p. 20.) In other cases, the opinion and record will not so clearly frame the issues, but a careful reading of the opinion and other documents should provide you with the important legal issues for the appeal.

Bell-Wesley v. O'Toole also presents several policy issues such as:

- Should society allow parents, who wish to keep their child, to force the doctor who negligently performed a vasectomy to pay for all of the costs that parents would normally incur in raising a child?

- What impact would that have on a child?

- On the medical profession?

- Would a decision against the doctor make it more difficult to find another doctor willing to perform a sterilization procedure?

- Were the parents actually traumatized by the birth, when in fact they had attempted to have children before opting for sterilization?

You need not, and probably cannot, determine all of the issues presented by the case before beginning to research. Indeed, in the course of library research you should continuously be refining issues and discovering new ways of looking at the case. Legal research is a dynamic process of moving from defining issues to developing arguments to finding support and then back again. Issues and arguments will inevitably be reformulated as you discover the content of statutes and case law.

4. Consider the Standard of Appellate Review. One issue you should consider as you read the record is the applicable standard of review. An appellate court invariably wants to know what elements of the trial court decision you want them to review. One common question asked by moot court judges is "Counsel, what is it that you want us to do here?" In most circumstances the standard of review will be mentioned in the record, generally as part of the questions certified for appeal. You should consider whether the appellate court is deciding issues de novo, considering whether there was an abuse of discretion by the trial judge or whether the factual findings were clearly erroneous, or whether governing law requires that the appellate court decide particular factual issues not addressed or improperly addressed in the court below. Your decision will likely have implications for both your written and oral advocacy. For example, if you are arguing that there was an abuse of discretion at the trial court level you may wish to argue that the appellate court decide the factual issues de novo. Thus, you will want to focus your arguments on the facts, perhaps at the expense of policy or legal arguments.

5. Formulate Arguments. The arguments you make in your written and oral presentation to the court answer the questions raised by the issues in your case. These arguments provide the reasons the court should find in your favor when resolving these issues.

Formulating arguments is a process, involving reason and analysis as well as reliance on authority. Before you go to the library to see how others have answered these questions, try to generate a list of answers yourself. Don't be afraid to rely on your intuition at first. Begin thinking of how you can best frame the arguments for (and against) the position that you wish to support. This list of sources will help generate some ideas:

- Arguments based on commonsense notions of justice and equity—often one's client got into a predicament through a good-faith belief about the correctness of a certain action;

- Arguments based on authorities and case law that you have already studied;

- Arguments by analogy or comparison to other cases and situations with which you are familiar;

- Arguments typically associated with the subject matter of the case;

- Arguments based on the potential consequences of the court's finding or not finding your way;

- Arguments affecting public policy.

This list is a starting point for research. During the course of your research you will of course discover new arguments to add to the list and reject some arguments as frivolous.

6. Connect the Facts to the Legal Issues. By now, you have a solid grasp of what actually happened and a basic understanding of the legal considerations. You should now synthesize the two sets of information. As will be discussed in Chapter IV, Writing the Brief, and Chapter VI, Oral Advocacy, the key to an effective argument will be your ability to relate the legal arguments to the specific factual situation.

This requires you to look critically at the information the record gives to determine which facts matter the most to your arguments. In this case, not every fact concerning Dr. O'Toole's performance of the vasectomy matters. Important facts are those that demonstrate how the wrongful birth of a child can be a real injury to the parents. Examples of the economic and emotional cost to Rebecca and Scott Bell-Wesley can be used for this purpose.

The process of relating the facts to the law helps you continually redefine the factual and legal issues. By evaluating the relationship between the two, you will begin to analyze critically both your factual and legal determinations. Your understanding of both areas will improve in the process.

7. Develop a Core Theory. After identifying the legal, factual, and policy issues, and generating a series of useful arguments, try to unite them into a single coherent thought, or "core theory." Typically, library work will be necessary before the theory crystallizes, but it will be helpful to formulate this theory before beginning your research.

The core theory presents the foundation of your position. It is the unifying theme of your argument around which all issues and questions are presented and arguments are formulated. It quite often consists of the overarching justifications for your position: the policy implications, the fairness considerations, and the proper role of the courts in deciding on this and similar issues arising in the future.

Developing the core theory takes time and thought. Throughout your work, think about the arguments you generate from the record and your research. Try to structure your ideas around a theory that captures the essence of your case. The more difficult task is articulating your core theory into a narrative of several words or sentences. Although it is not required to present your core theory in such a concise format in your brief, the process of distilling your ideas into a few sentences will produce the strand that connects your ideas into a cohesive whole.

Any case can give rise to a number of alternative core theories. Here are some examples of what a core theory could look like for the appellant and appellee in *Bell-Wesley v. O'Toole:*

Appellant:

Rebecca and Scott Bell-Wesley's wrongful birth claim is indistinguishable from any other medical malpractice claim. They must be compensated for all of the injuries flowing from Dr. O'Toole's repeated negligence and the resulting birth of a child after they had chosen to lead a childless lifestyle.

Appellee:

The Bell-Wesleys should not be awarded damages to pay for the costs of raising their son because they wanted a healthy child. They were not injured by his birth and therefore it would be wrong for Dr. O'Toole to compensate them for the birth of their healthy son.

8. Consider Opposing Arguments and Core Theories. As you begin the process of reading the record, formulating arguments, and developing a core theory, you should consider the arguments that the opposing party will make. Although the facts and legal issues are the same for both parties, the manner in which they are interpreted, developed, and eventually presented will differ.

A seemingly unambiguous fact might be subject to more than one interpretation, and varying inferences might be drawn from a given set of facts. The opposing party will present the facts and draw inferences in a light most favorable to its arguments. Likewise, they will select those arguments that most strongly support their core theory. Consider what that core theory might be and identify the possible arguments that make it work. By anticipating these opposing arguments and core theories now, you can identify weaknesses in your own arguments and core theory. Identifying weaknesses in your arguments and core theory might require you to strengthen and modify them appropriately.

It is not essential that you present arguments in your brief for each argument that the opposing party might marshal. Even if all the arguments are not included in your brief, they might be raised during oral argument.

9. Read the Rules. This is often a good time to familiarize yourself with the rules of your particular court, be it moot or authentic. Doing so now will avoid unnecessary rude shocks further down the line. The rules will supply information about deadlines and page limits, as well as format. Follow them carefully. While these guidelines are usually included with moot court documents, you should be aware that "real" rules are contained both in national compilations, such as the Federal Rules of Appellate Procedure, and local or circuit rules.

10. Read Through the Whole Record Again and Again, Until You Have a Firm Grasp of What It Contains. This is probably the most tedious step in the process, but its importance cannot be overemphasized. The more times you read through the record, the better your understanding of the facts will be. You may discover inconsistencies and omissions in the record as you become more and more familiar with it. The better you understand these problems, the better your ability will be to confront them.

A comprehensive understanding of the record—the factual, legal and policy issues—as well as the major arguments will facilitate the initial stages of research. That understanding will enable you to focus your research and plot a logical course of action. By simply rushing to the library without carefully considering the intricacies and nuances that are bound to exist in the record, you will probably find yourself exploring many unproductive paths. This is not to suggest that you should not modify your research strategy as you delve into the cases and references, but that your research will be more efficient and effective from the outset.

B. SAMPLE RECORD: BELL–WESLEY v. O'TOOLE

The sample moot court record for *Bell-Wesley v. O'Toole* appears on the following pages. Examine it carefully to see what documents it includes and what factual and legal issues it raises. Note especially that instructions on the last page limit the issues available to moot court participants; for example, whether the doctor's performance of the sterilization operation was negligent is not an issue. This type of constraint is common in moot court programs where skill development is more important than an exhaustive consideration of all possible issues.

Once you are familiar with the *Bell-Wesley v. O'Toole* record, you may want to compare your understanding of the facts and legal issues with the questions presented and the statements of the case in the sample briefs following Chapter IV.

*

COMPLAINT

SUPERIOR COURT FOR THE STATE OF AMES

REBECCA AND SCOTT BELL-WESLEY,
        Plaintiffs

        v.

DR. STEPHEN O'TOOLE,
        Defendant.

CIVIL ACTION 90-2004

COMPLAINT

JURISDICTION

1. Plaintiffs Rebecca and Scott Bell-Wesley are a married couple residing in the state of Ames.

2. Defendant Stephen O'Toole is a medical doctor who resides and has his medical office in the state of Ames.

CAUSES OF ACTION

3. Plaintiff Scott Bell-Wesley is an architect, under employment of the city of Holmes, City Planning Department.

4. Plaintiff Rebecca Bell-Wesley is an attorney, practicing with the state of Ames's Attorney General's office, in the city of Holmes.

5. Prior to January 4, 1990, plaintiff Rebecca Bell-Wesley had given birth to three deformed children, each of whom had died within six months after birth. Defendant O'Toole informed plaintiffs that there was a 75% chance that any child they conceived would suffer and die from the same congenital deformity.

6. Plaintiffs chose to lead a childless lifestyle by procuring a sterilization operation.

7. On October 16, 1988, defendant performed a vasectomy on plaintiff Scott Bell-Wesley for the purpose of preventing conception and birth of a child.

8. Defendant O'Toole was solely responsible for the performance of said operation, and for plaintiff's post-operative care.

9. Plaintiffs were advised by defendant that the operation would not render him sterile immediately, and that an alternative means of birth control should be used by plaintiffs until ten (10) weeks after the operation.

2

10. Plaintiffs used an alternate method of birth control for 3 months after Scott Bell-Wesley's vasectomy.

11. Plaintiffs were further informed by defendant O'Toole that a sperm count would have to be performed 12-14 weeks after the operation in order to determine the success of the operation.

12. Plaintiff Scott Bell-Wesley returned to the office of defendant O'Toole on January 8, 1989, at which time the defendant performed a sperm count and informed the plaintiff that he was sterile.

13. Plaintiff Rebecca Bell-Wesley was found to be pregnant on April 20, 1989 by defendant O'Toole.

14. Plaintiff Rebecca Bell-Wesley gave birth to Frank Michael Bell on January 4, 1990.

15. Plaintiff Scott Bell-Wesley is the biological father of Frank Michael Bell.

16. Defendant's separate acts of negligence were the proximate causes of the injury suffered by plaintiffs.

17. Plaintiffs were injured by the birth of their unplanned child.

18. Defendant's negligence has denied plaintiffs of their constitutionally protected right of self-determination in matters of childbearing.

19. Plaintiffs have incurred mental, physical, and financial injuries as a result of the conception and birth of their child, for which defendant is liable.

REMEDY

Wherefore, plaintiffs pray the court for the following relief:

20. That defendant be held liable to plaintiffs for the cost of Scott Bell-Wesley's vasectomy, including his medical expenses, his pain and suffering, and Rebecca's loss of consortium during his recuperation period in the amount of $10,000.

21. That defendant be held liable to plaintiffs for the medical expenses and pain and suffering caused by Rebecca Bell-Wesley's pregnancy and for Scott Bell-Wesley's loss of consortium during the last part of her pregnancy in the amount of $15,000.

22. That the defendant be held liable to plaintiff Rebecca Bell-Wesley for the medical expenses and pain and suffering

3

caused by her giving birth to Frank Michael Bell, in the amount of $25,000.

23. That defendant be held liable to plaintiffs for their emotional trauma caused by the conception and birth of an unplanned and unwanted child and for the additional emotional trauma resulting from plaintiffs' reasonable expectation that the child would suffer from a congenital deformity, in the amount of $100,000.

24. That the defendant be held liable to plaintiffs for lost earnings incurred as a result of Rebecca Bell-Wesley's pregnancy, and the birth and care of their child in the amount of $16,000 (see Trial Record, attached).

25. That the defendant be held liable to plaintiffs for injury to their lifestyle, which is impacted financially by the care and rearing of their child, and for their loss of control over their leisure hours, in the amount of $150,000. (see Exhibit A attached).

26. That the defendant be held liable to plaintiffs for the financial and emotional cost of rearing their child, in the amount of $250,000.

Plaintiffs further pray that the court order any additional measure of damages as would be just, and that provision for attorney's fees be made.

Respectfully submitted,

Scott and Rebecca Bell-Wesley
by their attorney

Jane E. Harvey
Llewellyn, Murray & Silber
325 North Bridge Road
Holmes, Ames

4

Exhibit A (in part)

From the 1989 annual report by the Dept. of Health and
Human Services, Washington, D.C.

The cost of raising a child, outside of possibly purchasing
a home, is the single greatest investment a family will
make. Current projections, stipulating that there is virtually
no limit on what a couple may invest, indicate that the very
minimum parents will spend bringing a child up to majority
will be $85,000. This figure includes the basic costs of
housing, feeding, and clothing the child, as well as the
minimum costs of maintaining his/her health up to age eighteen.
Addition of even several moderately priced "extras"--early
professional child care, private schooling, college, allowances
for serious illness--can push the cost of childrearing
beyond $150,000. And these figures do not yet even contemplate
the emotional costs of raising a child. . . .

5

SUPERIOR COURT FOR THE STATE OF AMES

REBECCA AND SCOTT BELL-WESLEY,
          Plaintiffs,

          v.

DR. STEPHEN O'TOOLE,
          Defendant.

CIVIL ACTION 90-2004

DEFENDANT'S ANSWER

1. Defendant admits the allegations in paragraphs 1-5 of plaintiffs' complaint.

2. Defendant denies the allegations in paragraph 6 of plaintiffs' complaint.

3. Defendant admits the allegations in paragraphs 7-14 of plaintiffs' complaint.

4. Defendant is without sufficient information to respond to paragraph 15 of plaintiffs' complaint.

5. Defendant denies the allegations in paragraphs 16-26 of plaintiffs' complaint.

FIRST AFFIRMATIVE DEFENSE

6. Plaintiffs assumed the risk of possible failure of the sterilization procedure.

7. Since even perfectly performed vasectomies are not successful in all cases (statistical rate of regrowth of the tubes) plaintiffs have assumed the risk of failure of the operation whether resulting from negligence or regrowth.

8. Since the social value of sterilization operations is so high, society has imposed this "assumption of risk" or waiver of recovery rights for those engaging in a procedure which cannot yet be made 100% effective, regardless of whether negligence was involved.

SECOND AFFIRMATIVE DEFENSE

9. Defendant was not negligent in his operative or post-operative procedures with plaintiff Scott Bell-Wesley.

10. Plaintiff Scott Bell-Wesley suffered a tubal regrowth which was a statistical failure of the procedure, not caused by defendant's negligence.

6

THIRD AFFIRMATIVE DEFENSE

11. The birth of a child is always a benefit and a blessing which outweighs any financial costs, as well as any pain and suffering incurred during pregnancy.

12. Where the parents' express purpose in procuring a vasectomy was to prevent the birth of a deformed child, the birth to the parents of a healthy child causes them no injury.

13. Therefore the plaintiffs did not suffer any damages and defendant is not liable to plaintiffs.

FOURTH AFFIRMATIVE DEFENSE

14. Broad social policies prohibit the awarding of damages in actions for wrongful birth.

15. Therefore, plaintiffs have failed to state a cause of action for which relief can be granted.

FIFTH AFFIRMATIVE DEFENSE

16. Plaintiffs have failed to mitigate the damages they suffered, by choosing not to terminate Rebecca Bell-Wesley's pregnancy by abortion.

17. Plaintiffs have additionally failed to mitigate the damages claimed in paragraph 23 of their complaint by refusing, as they have in the past, to undergo amniocentesis, a safe, simple test conducted early in the pregnancy which would have determined that child being carried was, and is, normal and healthy.

18. Plaintiffs have further failed to mitigate the damages in that they have not offered their "unwanted, unplanned" child up for adoption.

Respectfully submitted,

Dr. Stephen O'Toole
by his attorney

D. Nathan Neuville
Ericson, Swanson and Moses
1977 Pond Ave.
Holmes, Ames

7

Trial Record

(Parts have been omitted)

Counsel: Mrs. Bell-Wesley, what happened in the months
following the presumably successful sterilization
procedure?

Rebecca Bell-Wesley: Well, shortly after Scott's vasectomy
I accepted an offer from the Attorney General to
become one of his first assistant attorneys general.

Counsel: Are there many of these First Assistant Attorneys
General?

R.B.-W.: Oh, no. Just a handful--no more than four or
five, each located in a different city in Ames.

C: I see, and there is more involved in this than in
your prior position?

R.B.-W.: Yes, various department heads reported to me. I
also had considerable discretion over the policies
to be promulgated by our office as well as identifying
the goals sought through our litigation and authorizing
compromises and settlements.

C: You say had. Are you no longer in this position?

R.B.-W.: It's not clear. I have taken a six month leave of
absence, so I should return to work sometime in
May. In the meantime, many things could happen.
The Attorney General's is a political office, you
know.

C: And your position as Assistant Attorney General
was politically obtained?

R.B.-W.: No, the Attorney General usually only bothers
himself with hiring or bringing in his own first
assistants and department chiefs. I was hired out
of law school by a department chief at the time.

C: And what was your salary change upon acceptance of
your most recent position?

R.B.-W.: I went from $31,000/yr. to $47,000.

8

SUPERIOR COURT FOR THE STATE OF AMES

REBECCA AND SCOTT BELL-WESLEY,
    Plaintiffs,

      v.

DR. STEPHEN O'TOOLE,
    Defendant.

CIVIL ACTION 90-2004

FINDINGS OF FACT AND
CONCLUSIONS OF LAW

FINDINGS OF FACT

1. Plaintiffs made a conscious decision to avoid the possibility of the conception and birth of a child. The motive for this decision was their fear of having another deformed child.

2. In furtherance of this decision, Scott Bell-Wesley obtained a vasectomy from Dr. O'Toole on October 16, 1988.

3. Expert testimony showed that defendant failed to properly sever the tubes of the vas deferens, and the plaintiff was never rendered sterile.

4. Defendant negligently performed a sperm count and informed plaintiff Scott Bell-Wesley that he had been rendered sterile.

5. Defendant is a general practitioner medical doctor who has performed vasectomies in his office over the past few years.

6. Plaintiff Rebecca Bell-Wesley conceived and bore a child, Frank Michael Bell, on January 4, 1990.

7. Scott Bell-Wesley has been established to be the biological father. The pregnancy and childbirth were normal and without complications, except that they were unplanned; Frank Michael Bell was born healthy and has remained so since.

8. Plaintiffs declined to abort the child on moral grounds, and have declined to give the child up for adoption for various personal reasons.

9. Plaintiffs' lifestyle has changed dramatically since birth of the child.

10. Both parents have lost, and will continue to lose, time and wages in their chosen careers as a result of caring for the child.

9

11. Both parents profess a deep love for their child even though they bring the present action.

12. Expert testimony established that amniocentesis would have revealed that the fetus was not deformed and was in fact in good health.

10

CONCLUSIONS OF LAW

1. Defendant Dr. Stephen O'Toole performed a vasectomy on plaintiff Scott Bell-Wesley on October 16, 1988 which was unsuccessful.

2. Defendant O'Toole negligently performed a sperm count and informed plaintiff Scott Bell-Wesley that the operation was successful and he had been rendered sterile.

3. The conception and birth of plaintiffs' child would not have resulted had the operation been successful.

4. Plaintiffs have stated a cause of action for negligence.

5. Plaintiffs' damages are limited to the out of pocket costs, pain and suffering, and loss of consortium associated with Scott Bell-Wesley's vasectomy. A reasonable award for these damages is $10,000.

6. Damages are not awardable for the costs associated with pregnancy, birth, and rearing of a healthy child because the benefits of a healthy child always outweigh any attendant costs.

DATED: May 13, 1990   Signed

                                 _____

                                 NANCY LLEWENSTEIN

                                 Ames Superior Court Judge

11

SUPERIOR COURT OPINION

Llewenstein, J.

In this bench trial, we are faced with a difficult problem involving not only the rights of individuals, but also numerous social and systemic considerations as well. It is apparent to us that the operation was performed negligently. Not only was the operation itself ineffective, but the defendant was subsequently negligent in performing a sperm count on the plaintiff and in informing him, on the basis of this test, that he had been rendered sterile.

Yet plaintiffs allege that the birth of a healthy son must somehow be compensated by the defendant. The idea that a child would grow up being supported by another by virtue of the fact that his parents did not plan for or want him is, to us, repulsive. The very real inability to assign a dollar amount to such an "injury" is exceeded only by the harm which such an award could do to families and individuals in our society. Perhaps we are old-fashioned, but we are still filled with mystery, joy and inspiration at the birth of a new human life. In this case, where the plaintiffs' prior conceptions resulted in the birth and tragic deaths of three congenitally deformed infants, the birth to them of a healthy child is truly a blessing. The benefits of a healthy child clearly outweigh any and all associated costs, even those attributed to the unplanned pregnancy.

Scott Bell-Wesley's vasectomy was improperly performed and the post-operative care he received was inadequate. The defendant is liable for his improper medical treatment, and therefore damages of $10,000 are awarded to plaintiffs. However, we in Ames decline to join the ranks of jurisdictions recognizing a cause of action for wrongful birth. The benefits of a healthy child always outweigh any attendant costs or burdens. This case is no different.

12

SUPERIOR COURT FOR THE STATE OF AMES

REBECCA AND SCOTT BELL-WESLEY,
       Plaintiffs,

          v.

DR. STEPHEN O'TOOLE,
       Defendant.

CIVIL ACTION 90-2004

JUDGMENT

(JUDGMENT OF TRIAL COURT)

The issues in the above action having duly been heard by this court, and this court having made and filed its findings of fact and conclusions of law on May 13, 1990, it is, therefore,

ORDERED, ADJUDGED, AND DECREED, that judgment be entered for plaintiffs as to Defendant's acts of negligence and plaintiffs be awarded $10,000 in damages.

DATED: May 20, 1990   Signed

_____
          Clerk of Court

13

SUPERIOR COURT FOR THE STATE OF AMES

REBECCA AND SCOTT BELL-WESLEY,
             Plaintiffs,

                                    CIVIL ACTION 90-2004

           v.

                                    NOTICE OF APPEAL

DR. STEPHEN O'TOOLE,
             Defendant.

Notice is hereby given that Petitioners, Rebecca and Scott Bell-Wesley, appeal to the Supreme Court of the State of Ames, from the final judgment entered in this action on the 13th day of May, 1990

Dated: 21 May, 1990   Signed: _____
                                         Jane E. Harvey
                                         Attorney for Appellant (II)
                                         Llewellyn, Murray & Silber
                                         325 North Bridge Road
                                         Holmes, Ames

14

SUPERIOR COURT FOR THE STATE OF AMES

REBECCA AND SCOTT BELL-WESLEY,

      Plaintiffs,

        v.

DR. STEPHEN O'TOOLE,

      Defendant.

CIVIL ACTION 90-2004

STIPULATION OF THE RECORD

It is hereby stipulated by the attorneys for the respective parties in the above-named action, that the following shall constitute the transcript of the record on appeal.

1. Pleadings before the Superior Court of the State of Ames:

   a. Summons (omitted)

   b. Complaint

   c. Exhibit A

   d. Return of Service (omitted)

   e. Answer

   f. Affidavit of Service (omitted)

2. Trial Record

3. Findings of Fact & Conclusions of Law

4. Opinion of the Superior Court of the State of Ames

5. Judgment of the Superior Court of the State of Ames

6. Notice of Appeal

7. This Designation

15

INSTRUCTIONS TO PARTICIPANTS

Assume that no arguable issue exists concerning:

1. Plaintiffs' timeliness in bringing the action under the relevant statute of limitations.

2. Defendant's negligence in performing the operation and in performing the sperm count upon which he relied in informing plaintiff Scott Bell-Wesley he was sterile.

3. The actual amount of damages as a goal upon appeal. Quantification and award of each element is determined upon remand; the issue then is whether the court should recognize each type of damage as recoverable.

Chapter III

RESEARCHING THE BRIEF

Once you are familiar with the record, and you have given some consideration to a core theory, you are ready to begin your research. The basic objective of legal research is to find support from "authorities" ("sources") to strengthen your position. "Binding" or "mandatory" authorities are those that must be followed by all lower courts and administrative bodies in that jurisdiction. "Persuasive" authorities are those that may carry a great deal of weight because of the body or person that created them, but need not be followed in the jurisdiction in which you are working.

The stronger the authority, the better, but relevance without strength is better than strength without relevance.

Here is what you will find in this chapter:
A. TYPES OF LEGAL RESEARCH SOURCES
B. FEATURES OF INDIVIDUAL SOURCES
C. HOW TO USE THESE SOURCES
D. DATA BASES AND COMPUTERIZED RESEARCH
E. TIPS FOR RESEARCHING
F. FINAL REMARKS

It is impossible in one small chapter to go into full detail on how to use individual publications or data bases. For more specific information, please consult a reference librarian or the books listed below, many of which may be on reserve or in the reference area. For an excellent overview emphasizing the process of legal research for beginners, see C. Wren and J. Wren, *The Legal Research Manual* (2d ed. 1986).

For more extended descriptions on individual books and data bases, see M. Cohen, *Legal Research in a Nutshell* (4th ed. 1985); M. Cohen, R. Berring & K. Olson, *Finding the Law* (1989); J. Jacobstein and R. Mersky, *Fundamentals of Legal Research* (5th ed. 1990).

Many law school libraries have available free pamphlets from some of the major publishers. Ask whether your school has pamphlets from the West Publishing Co., the Lawyers Co-operative Publishing Co., and Shepard's Citations (Shepard's/McGraw-Hill). These well illustrated pamphlets will flesh out many of the details we can not go into here.

A. TYPES OF LEGAL RESEARCH SOURCES

Sources can be divided into four very general categories:

(1) Primary sources (the law itself);

(2) Secondary sources (summaries or analyses of the law);

(3) Finding aids; and

(4) Legally related materials from other disciplines.

B. FEATURES OF INDIVIDUAL SOURCES

1. Primary Sources. Primary sources are actual law in their jurisdiction. In the American system, there are numerous primary sources, including the U.S. Constitution and state constitutions. Congress and state legislatures create statutory law. Federal and state courts, by issuing opinions, create case law. (Note that court opinions are often interpretations of law derived from the other sources.) Federal and state agencies create regulations and also issue rulings in adjudications that fall into the category of administrative law.

Primary sources are the strongest and most important sources for your argument. Frequently, as you examine the various primary sources, you will find that those who make law often disagree with each other. It is important to sort out the relationships, if any, between the various authorities to see whether one has preference over the others. For example, federal sources take precedence over state ones in issues involving "federal questions."

Although some limited amount of publishing for primary sources is still done by the federal and state governments, most legal materials come from commercial publishers. Individual statutes and decisions are often first issued by governments in pamphlet form known as "slip laws" or "slip decisions," respectively. They are then cumulated chronologically into bound volumes. Between the individual slip law or decision and the final bound volume, sometimes interim pamphlets, known as "advance sheets," are available as preprints using the page numbering of the forthcoming volume.

Chronological volumes of statutes are known generically as "session laws," i.e., laws passed at each session of a legislative body. The federal session laws are known as the *Statutes-at-Large*.

Chronological volumes of decisions are known as "reports" or "reporters." Formerly, every state issued "official," i.e., governmentally published, reports of their highest court and sometimes of any intermediate level of appellate court. Today less than half of the states continue that practice.

The official decisions of the Supreme Court of the United States are known as *United States Reports* ("U.S."). The West Publishing Co.'s version is the *Supreme Court Reporter* ("S.Ct.") and the Lawyers Cooperative Publishing Co.'s set is called the *Lawyers Edition* ("L.Ed."). *United States Law Week* is probably the most widely used weekly publication reporting the most important decisions at federal and state levels. It is most often used for its U.S. Supreme Court section which prints cases before they appear in the advance sheets of *Supreme Court Reporter* or *Lawyers Edition.*

Whenever you see the name or initials of the jurisdiction, you know it is the court of last resort. For example, "301 U.S. 411" means the case begins on page 411 of volume 301 of the reports of the U.S. Supreme Court. NOTE: Many reporters are into a second or higher numbered series, e.g., "74 F.2d 324." That indicates the case is in volume 74 of the second series (not second edition) of chronological volumes of the Federal Reporter which deals with the courts of appeals.

Obviously, it would be impractical to search through the indexes of individual volumes of statutes, regulations, and cases to find what is still good law. For that reason, tools were developed having broad subject access to primary legal materials allowing the user to take into account amendments and rescissions to statutes and regulations. Likewise, search tools were designed to track later decisions which may have modified earlier decisions or commented on statutes or regulations.

Compilations of currently valid statutes or regulations arranged in a subject fashion are known generically in this country as "codes." The federal statutory code is called the *United States Code* ("U.S.C."). The West Publishing Co. has a case annotated version known as *United States Code Annotated* ("U.S.C.A.") and the Lawyers Co-operative Publishing Co. also produces an annotated version known as *United States Code Service* ("U.S.C.S."). There are statutory codes for each of the states.

2. Secondary Sources. Many moot court cases require you to write and speak intelligently on legal topics in which you have no expertise. This problem is not unique to moot court; when you leave law school, there will still be areas of the law about which you know nothing. When you need to learn about a legal area quickly, secondary sources can provide you with important background information.

Secondary sources comment on primary sources and often provide texts from such primary authorities. Although you cannot expect to find all of the required answers to a given legal problem in secondary sources, they are very helpful starting points. They are most useful not so much as restatements of the law itself, but for discussions of how a particular area has developed, how it should develop, or how it is likely to change.

In addition to providing helpful background information, a chapter in a hornbook (one volume treatise for students) or a law review article is particularly good in summarizing arguments made in support of or against cases that you may find relevant. They generally direct you to important cases on the topic which can save you an enormous amount of time.

Secondary sources are often cited in legal arguments and opinions. The strength of secondary sources varies greatly, and usually is a direct function of the status of the particular author or publication.

The principal secondary sources are listed below:

(a) Restatements of the Law;

(b) Law Reviews;

(c) Treatises;

(d) Legal Encyclopedias;

(e) American Law Reports annotations; and

(f) Bar journals and legal newspapers.

a. Restatements of the Law. Of these sources, only the Restatements of the Law on basic "common law" topics have achieved quasi-primary status. The Restatements are often cited in legal arguments and opinions. The individual Restatements were authored by committees of prominent scholars associated with the American Law Institute.

The laws of agency, contracts, torts, property, trusts, judgments, and conflict of laws have been "restated." Generally, the Restatements do not carry as much weight as primary sources; however, many states have declared the common law as summarized in the Restatements to be law in their jurisdictions unless contrary to declared public policy.

b. Law Reviews. Law reviews are periodicals produced at law schools and typically edited by students. They contain articles, notes, case comments and book reviews written by professors, practitioners, judges, and students. Law review articles are even cited by the U.S. Supreme Court on what the law should be.

c. Treatises. Treatises vary in size from one volume student texts to multi-volume sets. Some authors have written for several audiences, producing the one volume introductory text as well as editing a major treatise. Some treatises are in looseleaf format (see the discussion at p. 32 "Format").

d. Legal Encyclopedias. Legal encyclopedias provide general discussions of virtually any legal subject. The two most common encyclopedias are *Corpus Juris Secundum* ("C.J.S."), and *American Jurisprudence 2d* ("Am. Jur.2d"). The national encylopedias in trying to summarize the law of all states rely almost solely on case law. They essentially ignore the enormous amount of relevant state statutory law apart from Uniform or Model laws which may have been adopted by many states.

C.J.S. is produced by West Publishing Co. and Am. Jur.2d by Lawyers Co-operative Publishing Co. ("Co-op"). Each publisher ties its set into its own family of publications. In C.J.S. you will find references to the West system of case law digests (discussed at p. 33 "Digests"). Similarly, in Am. Jur.2d, Co-op lists references to one of its major publications, *American Law Reports,* discussed in the next section.

There are also encyclopedias designed for those states where the bar is large enough to sustain such a market. Notable examples are *New York Jurisprudence 2d* and *Texas Jur. III.* State legal encyclopedias are often quite useful because of their references not only to case but to statutory law.

Encyclopedias are written in a discursive or narrative style. Each clause or sentence is usually justified with specific references to case law from all states. This narrative feature is their chief advantage over the disjointed look of case law digests (discussed at p. 30 "Digests"); digests are a highly organized collection of individual paragraphs each of which summarize a point of law in a particular case.

Legal encyclopedias are good for background reference but remember that your ultimate goal for the brief is to find primary sources: the law itself.

e. American Law Reports. Co-op publishes *American Law Reports* ("A.L.R.") which reprints a highly selective group of significant cases. Following each case is an "annotation," a synopsis of all American law on that narrow topic. Researchers use A.L.R. not for the case itself but rather for the annotation which follows.

f. Bar Journals. With few exceptions, articles appearing in bar journals are not scholarly in nature. Such journals, along with legal newspapers, can be quite useful in producing, information on brand new topics not covered elsewhere. Generally, articles in bar journals and legal newspapers are designed for current awareness and not for in-depth analysis.

3. Finding Aids. "Finding aids" lead you to primary and secondary sources but do not provide either the text of the law or any discussion of it. The chief "finding aids" are the following:

(a) *Shepard's Citations,*

(b) the West digest system, and

(c) periodical indexes.

a. Shepard's Citations. *Shepard's Citations* is the principal way for you to find out whether the authority you are interested in is still good law. Shepard's provides information on how *later* authorities treat the "basic" or "cited" authority (statute, case, regulation, law review article). Although the vast majority of Shepard's information is prospective in nature, it does list the history of a case on appeal giving lower court citations.

b. Digests. Digests provide subject access to case law through alphabetically arranged topics and numbered subtopics of abstracts of points of law from all reported cases covered by that particular digest.

c. **Periodical indexes.** You can find law reviews or legal newspapers dealing with your topic by consulting legal periodical indexes, similar to the *Readers' Guide to Periodical Literature.*

4. Legally Related Materials From Other Disciplines. On occasion, nonlegal materials from fields bearing on the law are very useful, e.g., statistics, economics, and social sciences. For example, materials from the physical and biological sciences may be helpful in areas such as environmental law.

C. HOW TO USE THESE SOURCES

Seldom will one issue lead you to a single publication and a definitive answer. It is useful to think of the various publications as part of a large, interconnected system. Normally, you will find only a part of your total argument in any one source. There are many paths from many points to many answers, and you can usually get from any place within the system to any other place, so long as you use the tools properly.

You should be aware that the order in which the various tools are discussed is of no particular significance. Which tool you begin with depends upon the nature of the question and the relative amount of expertise you bring to the topic you are researching. If you are relatively unfamiliar with the topic, then you may want to find a general overview first.

The Restatements of the Law, legal encyclopedias, and treatises contain summaries of the law from a broad perspective. They are useful in developing a working knowledge of the topic. Law review articles are generally written from a single perspective and often advance and support arguments on what the state of the law in an area should be.

Sometimes, it is quite clear which source you need to consult first. For example, if you merely wish to find the elements of criminal fraud in a particular jurisdiction, you may go directly to that jurisdiction's criminal code. If, however, you wish to determine how those elements have been interpreted by the courts in that jurisdiction, you will have to extend your search to court opinions.

How you proceed from your first source depends on how much information you got from it. There may be specific references to other sources or you may have to choose another source and use its index to find out how that question is categorized in that specific publication. In the absence of specific leads from the first tool used, your selection of the next source will depend on what you think is likely to lead you to further information in as comprehensive and efficient a manner as possible. As you become more experienced, that choice will become much easier.

Most law students and lawyers quickly learn the arrangement of federal and state primary sources in their library. Likewise, most soon become acquainted with the location of the main finding aids (Shepard's, digests, and indexes) as well as the national legal encyclopedias and dictionaries. There is usually a fairly clear pattern based on jurisdiction and within that by type of publication.

1. Format. Certain types of legal publications are designed to be permanent in nature. Examples are decisional volumes, law reviews, and many treatises. With the last example, a new edition may or may not be forthcoming.

There are other materials which are to be regularly supplemented. Among them are statutory codes, digests, some treatises, and encyclopedias. Many of these sets have a slit in the inside back cover into which a cumulative supplement, called a "pocket part", fits. The pocket part, usually issued annually, contains changes to the text in the main volume along with references to recently published sources. When the pocket part becomes too thick to fit into the back cover, the publisher often issues a free standing pamphlet until the next full scale revision of that volume integrating the pocket part information into the main volume.

Certain specialized materials are issued in a "looseleaf" format. These materials are supplemented when publishers send the users new pages with instructions to remove older no longer current material. Most practitioners and faculty members depend heavily on looseleaf materials to keep current in their fields. The availability of a "looseleaf service" devoted to your topic may significantly reduce your efforts. Consult the subject index of *Legal Looseleafs In Print* to see whether your library owns any for your topic.

2. Statutes. In order to find statutes, locate the statutory code for the jurisdiction in which you are interested. If there is a case annotated commercial version, use that one for research purposes. It may even be more current than any official version. Look up your subject in the code index. If your subject is governed by statutory law, there will be a reference to (a) particular statutory section(s). You then simply look up the section(s) in the code. Remember to check the pocket part in both the index and the code—legislatures often pass laws on new subjects and often change or repeal old laws.

3. Regulations. Finding federal regulations is similar to finding statutes. The commercial indexes are preferred for subject searching. The official index has an excellent table going from U.S. Code statutory citations to any Code of Federal Regulations issued under authority of those statutory sections.

At the state level, many administrative codes are in looseleaf format. Unfortunately, indexes for state codes are rarely published. The state administrative codes are often organized under the agencies issuing the regulations. You generally must guess which agency or agencies control your area of interest.

4. The West "National Reporter System" for Case Law. "Reporter" volumes are chronological collections of court decisions, almost entirely at the appellate level. The West Publishing Co. publishes separate reporters for each level of the federal courts and reporters for "regions" (geographical groupings of states) plus separate reporters for New York and California as well as a few topical ones.

Here is a list of the main West units:

- Supreme Court Reporter
- Federal Reporter [Court of Appeals for all circuits]
- Federal Supplement [district courts, i.e., federal trial courts]
- Federal Rules Decisions
- Atlantic Reporter
- North Eastern Reporter
- North Western Reporter
- Pacific Reporter
- South Eastern Reporter
- South Western Reporter
- Southern Reporter

5. Digests. West's "digests" provide a topical approach to those cases by abstracting points of law found in specific case reporters. There are digests for individual states, the regional reporters, the federal courts in general, a special one for the U.S. Supreme Court, and separate ones for the topical reporters. There are four simple steps to follow in using the West system:

(a) Make a subject and jurisdiction determination;

(b) Look up the subject(s) in the *Descriptive Word Index* to the digest to obtain the digest topic name and "key number" (numbered subtopic);

(c) Follow the reference in the index to the case digest; read the case summaries in the digest and then record the citations of all relevant cases; and

(d) Use the citations to find the fully printed cases in the reporters.

a. Subject and Jurisdiction Determination. You must begin by determining the legal subjects you wish to research and the jurisdictions in which you wish to focus that research. Find the digests that deal with your jurisdictions. For example, in *Bell-Wesley v. O'Toole,* you would be most interested in state law because the wrongful birth tort is covered by state law. Any case heard in federal court because of diversity jurisdiction will be included in a state digest covering the state law that the federal court was interpreting. However, the case itself would appear in a federal reporter.

Because Ames is a mythical jurisdiction, counsel in *Bell-Wesley v. O'Toole* would be interested in the laws of many states. If, however, the case was in an Arizona court, counsel could go directly to the Arizona Digest or the Pacific Reporter Digest which includes Arizona. As with any regional reporter digest, it abstracts case law from only those states covered by that regional reporter. Where there is no state digest, there is a regional, and vice versa.

Above the state, regional, federal and specialized digests are the overarching Decennial and General Digests of which the others are subsets.

Through the Eighth Decennial, the Decennials were true ten-year cumulations of all federal and state cases in the West system. With the Ninth, the so-called "Decennial" was divided into two separate cumulations, Part One and Part Two, each covering a five year period.

To supplement the five year cumulations, West issues a volume of the General Digest about every six weeks. Assuming you have found a West digest topic and key number you are satisfied with in the latest "Decennial" five year cumulation, carry over that topic and key number into the General Digest. Each General Digest volume is a self-contained unit covering all topics from A to Z. To save you from having to examine each General Digest volume, every tenth volume (10th, 20th, etc.) has cumulative indexes and a table showing which volumes, if any, in those ten volumes contain abstracts on that topic and key number.

b. Descriptive Word Index. The Descriptive Word Index is an alphabetical listing of topics located at the end of each set of digest volumes. The index contains both legal concepts and fact words, e.g., negligence and swimming pool.

With *Bell-Wesley* in mind, you could search under legal concepts, such as "Wrongful Birth" or "Wrongful Life," as well as fact words like "Vasectomy." For example, under "Wrongful Birth," you will find, in slightly darker print, the entry "Phys 18.110." This entry is the topic name ("Phys," which stands for "Physicians and Surgeons") and key number (18.110) for your subject. Record this information. [For a parallel path, see Illustration #1 at the end of this chapter for the entry under "Vasectomy" in the *Ninth Decennial Digest*, Part 2, 1981–1986.]

c. Digest. Now turn to the digest volumes proper. Topics in the digests are arranged in alphabetical order by topic name and then subarranged in numerical order by key number. In this example, you should turn to the volume containing the topic "Physicians and Surgeons" and find the entries for key number 18.110. There is a collection of abstracts of cases relevant to your inquiry. You should also check the pocket part to see whether any pertinent cases have been decided more recently.

A digest search might have turned up an abstract for a point of law addressed in *Ramey v. Fassoulas,* 414 So.2d 198 (Fla.1982). *Ramey* states that parents who have a healthy child cannot be said to be damaged in a wrongful birth claim. This case appears to discuss directly one of the issues determined at the very beginning of the research process. [See Illustration #2 at the end of this chapter for *Ramey* under Physicians and Surgeons 18.110 in the *Ninth Decennial Digest*, Part 2, 1981–1986.]

 d. Reporters. Finally, use the citations to find the fully printed cases in the reporters. In our example, you would find *Ramey v. Fassoulas* in the Southen Reporter, Second Series ("So.2d"), volume 414 at page 198. Many students wonder why it is necessary to read the entire case after having read the case summary in the digest. Simply put, the case summaries are prepared by the West staff, and not by the court issuing the opinion. Consequently, although they are usually accurate, they cannot be considered statements of the law. Absolutely never cite a case without reading all of it. Headnotes cannot capture critical nuances. Be sensitive to how each case could be distinguished and differentiated on the basis of its facts. [See Illustration #3 at the end of this chapter for the first page of the *Ramey* case. Note that the abstracts in the digest were exact reprints of the two headnotes, both classified under Physicians and Surgeons 18.110.]

6. Shepard's Citations. *Shepard's Citations* are enormous lists showing how later legal sources have treated earlier sources. The main idea of Shepard's is to find out whether any later authorities have mentioned or "cited" the basic document whose status you are checking: statute, regulation, case, etc. It enables you to determine the relevance of those later authorities to the issue you are researching by seeing how they have treated your original source. Apart from listing the history of a case on appeal, Shepard's brings you forward in time—to discussions nearer the present day.

Analogous to a book review index, Shepard's tells you where you can read a "review" of the legal authority you have in hand. You must still go to that review and read it yourself. Unlike such an index, however, it often gives you some hints as to whether those "reviews" were favorable or not.

Shepard's Citations are used for two distinct purposes. The first and most crucial use of Shepard's is to determine whether those cases on which you intend to rely are still valid law, i.e., they have not been reversed on appeal, or the principles of law on which they were decided have not been overruled, or their value has not been vitiated by later decisions. This function is the single most important task a researcher must perform. Of all legal research tasks, this must be done with the greatest care. Failure to Shepardize properly is tantamount to legal malpractice!

Second, Shepard's is a marvelous case finder. This is especially true early on in your search when you may have only a single cite to begin with. You can quickly expand your horizons by finding a number of cases that have mentioned your original case.

The basic techniques for Shepardizing are very much the same for any source being Shepardized. In our example below, we will focus on Shepardizing case law. Although there are Shepard's units for statutes and regulations in addition to case citators, Shepard's is most often consulted for updating case law. One reason is that annotated statutory codes provide an alternative route for finding cases which have cited statutes.

To begin you should have a specific citation to a case in one of the West reporters. In general, non-West cites must first be converted to a parallel West cite to use Shepard's. Where this is not possible, you may want to use either one of the two national on-line data bases in lieu of Shepard's to find cites to your case (see p. 40 "Data Bases and Computerized Research" for discussions of on-line data bases.)

Assume that during your research you discovered a New York opinion which supported your argument. You want to determine whether it is still valid law. At the same time you would like to find other cases which have cited the opinion and which presumably would support your position. The citation for your original case is 301 N.Y.S.2d 519. You should follow these four steps.

a. Locate the proper set of Shepard's citators. Shepard's has citators corresponding to each of the reporter systems in which a case may be cited, i.e. official reporters, unofficial reporters, specialty reporters, etc. Shepard's also has citators chronicling treatment of the United States Constitution, federal statutes, federal regulations, and the Restatements of the Law.

For this example, you should find a set of citators that covers the New York Supplement (Second Series), beginning with the first citator volume in which volume 301 of the New York Supplement is listed. You need to refer to the citator volume or paperback supplement in which your authority could first possibly appear plus all subsequent volumes or supplements in which the authority might continue to be listed. Many Shepard's units are updated monthly. Gold pamphlets usually indicate a semi-annual supplement, red often quarterly or monthly, and white ones monthly.

On the cover of each paperback is a list of all volumes and pamphlet supplements you need to have a complete search for your case. You should come to Shepard's having read your case and written down the *year* of its decision. Each Shepard's volume has a date on its spine. Knowing the year of the decision will allow you to choose which volume or pamphlet might have the first possible entry for your original case. It is important to remember that the volumes and supplements are not cumulative; you must look in each one.

b. Look up the cite in the citator. For this example, you should look up volume 301 of the second series of New York Supplement, page 519 in the citator. Since many reporters are into a second or subsequent numbered series, be careful that you have noted the series number correctly at the top. First series are not actually designated "first" on either the reporter volume itself or in Shepard's. For example, the first series of the New York Supplement was simply called "New York Supplement." To find parallel citations for your basic case, look to the earliest possible volume. [See Illustration #4 at the end of this chapter.]

c. Check to see whether the case been reversed, overruled, or otherwise weakened in its effect. This is done by referring to the small letters to the left of the list of citations. These letters are abbreviations Shepard's uses to indicate how the original case has been treated. A list of Shepards' abbreviations and their meanings is found at the front of every Shepard's citator. The letter "r" means the original case was reversed on appeal. This is a perfect example of why it is so important to actually read that later case since your basic or cited case may have been reversed on other grounds.

Right after decisions related to the appellate history of the basic case follow other cases not a part of the original litigation. The vast majority of citations in Shepards are of this second type.

The most important symbol among this second group would be "o" which means the cited case overruled the original case. You should read the citing case since you don't know whether the basic case was overruled or on which point of law.

Many researchers merely look for any reversal or overruling in a quick and dirty manner of Shepardizing. Carried to an extreme, that practice can be quite dangerous. At least check all cases with treatment letters which might cast doubt on the case's status as precedent, such as those which stand for the following: distinguished, criticized, limited, questioned or explained. Of particular importance are cases preceded by "d"; that means the citing case has distinguished itself from the cited case on the basis of the facts or the law.

d. Use the notations to find supporting authority. In order to find support for the position taken by the original case, look for the letter "f" which means the later case followed the principle announced in the original case. In addition, check out those which have "h" ("harmonized") or "p" ("parallel"—substantially alike or the same in its law or facts).

Most entries do not have letters before them. No notation can mean one of two things. The first possible reason for no notation is Shepard's did not feel the court had given a clear indication how it felt about the earlier case, leaving it to you the reader to figure out.

The second possibility is that the case was cited in passing as authority for one of its principles of law without the later court at that point stating whether or not it accepts the law in the earlier case. Later on in that case, it may follow, reject, or modify that rule and cite your original case again. If it does, Shepard's will then precede that cite with a letter.

To increase the precision of your Shepard's research, take the West headnotes from your original case, and restrict your search to cites which have mentioned only the portion of the original case which interests you. For example, if the second headnote in the case that you are Shepardizing dealt with applying the benefits rule to a wrongful birth case, and that was the only part of the case that interested you, you could look in the citator for all cites to that case which have a tiny superscript "2" (looks like an exponent) listed after the reporter abbreviation. That means that the later court specifically cited the case for that issue, i.e., the issue raised in headnote "2," the benefits rule issue. This technique can save needless hours of chasing down cites that are not relevant to the issue that you are researching.

At the end of the list of citations you may find a number of citations to law review articles and A.L.R. annotations that have mentioned the case.

So long as you are only checking the continuing validity of the same case, you may stop at step c. listed above. The final step is used to direct you to other relevant sources. Be aware that the letter notations are extremely narrow with respect to what they can convey.

7. Shepardizing U.S. Supreme Court Cases. The neophyte often pales when Shepardizing a major constitutional case. For example, for *Griswold v. Connecticut*, 381 U.S. 479 (1965), Shepard's lists over 3,000 cases citing it in its official reports version.

A comprehensive Shepardizing session should include not only the official but also the two commercial versions. [In a similar manner, you should Shepardize both official and unofficial versions of state cases.] Since it takes about two years before even the advance sheets of the U.S. Reports come out, citations in the interim will be to the two unofficial reporters. All three sets provide citations from federal courts. There are differences, however. The chief one is that citations to state court cases are found only under the official reports version.

To help you sort through the citations, start by matching the headnote number for the issue you are researching with the superscript numbers in the citations of citing cases.

After you have completed the superscript method, there is another strategem available. Shepard's presents its citations in a clearly hierarchical fashion: first come Supreme Court cites, then you will find the federal circuits in numerical order. Within each circuit, you will first find Court of Appeals cases followed by district court decisions. After that appear cases from the states in alphabetical order by state. Within each group, the order of citations is by volume number of the reporting series and thus essentially chronological. After paying special attention to any citations by the Supreme Court itself, try taking several of the latest decisions from each circuit of the Court of Appeals.

8. Legal Periodical Indexes. Law review articles can be retrieved through two indexes: the *Index to Legal Periodicals* ("I.L.P.") and the *Current Law Index* ("C.L.I."). Both publications list articles according to author, subject, name of statute or case. In addition, they both index book reviews. The "advance sheets" (paper supplements) are issued about once a month and cumulated into annual bound volumes. You should examine each advance sheet after the last bound volume. Since some moot court topics are often brand new, how far back you go depends on how much you retrieve among the last few years worth. Remember the further back you go to find cases in any legal source, the longer the process of Shepardizing those cases may be. There is a fraternal twin to the *Current Law Index* called the *Legal Resources Index*. This microform index cumulates the annual volumes of the C.L.I. In addition, it has references to legal newspapers which often contain material on new areas of the law.

9. American Law Reports. The multivolume *Index to Annotations* indexes A.L.R. annotations from the second through the current fourth series, the A.L.R. Federal series, and annotations which occasionally appear following cases in the Lawyers Edition of the U.S. Supreme Court Reports. Once you have retrieved an A.L.R. volume, check the pocket part for any updates to annotations in that volume. In addition, the *Index to Annotations* also has a table showing which annotations have been supplemented or superseded by later annotations.

The main way you get into A.L.R. is through Shepardizing a case. If the case you are checking in Shepard's has been chosen to be reprinted in A.L.R., it will be followed by an annotation. The A.L.R. citation is listed in Shepard's right after identifying page number which introduces the column of citations—in the space for parallel citations to your base case. If the case you are interested in is mentioned in an A.L.R. annotation, then it will always appear as the very last citation in a Shepard's list. You should take a look at the end of the list of citations to whether there is a citation to an A.L.R. annotation.

D. DATA BASES AND COMPUTERIZED RESEARCH

Many lawyers today rely on the speed and accuracy of computerized data bases in both the exploratory and final stages of their research. Because a computer can search rapidly through its vast storage capacity in response to a search command, computer-aided research can quickly and effectively augment traditional research methods. For example, it is easy to request opinions written by a particular judge or in a particular circuit on a specific topic. Since data bases are kept very current, computer searches are especially helpful for updating and for investigating newly emerging areas of the law.

On-line searching is ideal when you want to combine two or more concepts or facts, a process that is often impossible using the unilinear approaches of traditional hard copy indexes. Generally, on-line searches are best when the facts are very specific or the issues quite narrow. When you are searching for broad overviews, hard copy secondary sources are preferrable because computer searches dredge up too much to be reviewed effectively.

Even though law libraries and many law firms have access to either or both of the two major legal data bases, Westlaw and Lexis, students still need to learn traditional legal research methods. Here are some of the reasons:

- Many older materials are not on-line.

- You may not always have immediate access to the data base or some mechanical problem prevents access. You should know how to use the equivalent hard copy materials as an alternative.

- First learning the individual features of each research tool in hard copy makes it much easier to deal with the on-line version.

- Traditional research is also more cost effective for certain types of research.

- Each system has its own training program, available through libraries, subscribers, or the company itself, and those programs are the only way to learn the best research strategies. There are also many other specialized legal data bases as well as legally related ones which may be available at your library.

E. TIPS FOR RESEARCHING

- Organize your notes by the issues. Even though you may be interested in only one issue that a case raises, take good notes on the context in which that particular issue is raised. Jotting down all the basic information while you are reading the case will prevent repeated visits to the same source. Even the most trustworthy memory won't be able to keep the facts of the umpteenth case straight.

- Mark your trail well. Make sure to write down parallel cites, numbers of pages from which you have extracted quotations, and other data that are infinitely easier to record while the source is in front of you than while the word processor is humming with your final brief in it.

- One way to be reasonably certain you have touched all relevant cases is to read cases cited in other cases until you start finding the same cases cited over and over again. Until then, continue to check all the customary sources.

- Having found case notes following a statutory section in a code or reference from a statutory Shepard's, you must determine what the text of the statute was when the court made its decision. It may make a difference as to the current relevance of the holding. Historical notes concerning any amendments often follow the code section; they should allow you to recreate the exact text.

- Cases dealing with newly developing legal issues are often first put under old digest topics which might not seem appropriate to you. All the more reason to make sure you have thought of all possible ways the "descriptive word index" might have dealt with it in the absence of a brand new topic. When you get to the actual digest topic, first take a look at the outline preceding the topic. Check the key numbers following and preceding yours to find out whether nearby key numbers might also be useful. It is analogous to fine-tuning an FM radio.

- Recognize the importance of being up-to-date. Familiarize yourself with the specific way any particular source is updated, like pocket parts. Always Shepardize those sources on which your argument will finally rest. *Know the rules* of your court governing the use of brand-new or unreported authority. If electronic sources are permitted for your moot court, use Lexis and Westlaw as ad hoc citators. In addition, Shepard's are available on both systems. Shepard's Preview for the most recent cases is available on Westlaw.

- Use of subject-oriented publications (usually secondary sources) can save you much time. In the absence of such sources, you will have to do research in the general sources we have described.

- For sample briefs and oral argument, see whether your library subscribes to a hard copy series entitled *Landmark Briefs and Arguments of the Supreme Court of the United States.* Alternatively, many libraries receive records and briefs as well as transcripts of oral argument in microform format.
- Let's review which sources can lead you to cases:
- Cases themselves cite to other cases.
- Cases in the West system of reporters are preceded by headnotes, each of which is classified by a digest topic name and key number for the subtopic. You can then go to any digest using that name and key number to find other cases on the same legal point.
- Case annotations following the text of a section in commercial editions of statutory codes. (Note also that *United States Code Annotated* ("U.S.C.A.") and many of the state statutory codes are published by West, and therefore have references to the West key number system.)
- Footnotes to encyclopedias, treatises, and law reviews, as well as textual references in American Law Reports annotations.
- The majority of citations in most Shepard's Citations units are to cases which have mentioned your cited legal authority.

F. FINAL REMARKS

This has been only a brief introduction to legal research. We highlighted only those research tools most frequently used by students in moot courts. We should mention areas we did *not* cover:

> Legal dictionaries or "Words and Phrases";
>
> Tables which convert from the chronological arrangements of statutes or regulations to their respective subject arrangements, i.e., codes;
>
> Materials which constitute the legislative history of statutes which are often useful when arguing legislative intent;
>
> How to find administrative decisions; and
>
> Research materials in specific areas of the law.

There simply is not enough space to go into such detail. For that reason, consult more extensive treatments given in those books listed at the beginning of this chapter.

By treating the various tools as part of an overall system of legal information, you can create a research strategy that will lead you to your ultimate goal: the primary sources of the law relevant to the issue you are researching.

Given the same problem, any two researchers, even seasoned ones, may begin using different tools. Although a disinterested observer might suggest that one method might be more efficient or comprehensive than another, the researchers' initial choices are determined by how much expertise they have with the topic and their individual experience with the legal research materials for that area.

Although much of this will seem complicated at first, rest assured that by following the steps outlined above for each tool you will become an effective and efficient legal researcher.

ILLUSTRATION #1

VALUE—Cont'd
IMPROVEMENTS—
Damages for breach of covenant of
warranty. **Covenants 130(6)**
Recovery for breach of covenant of sei-
sin. **Covenants 125(5)**
INCHOATE right of dower. **Dower & C
32**
INCOME tax, see this index **Income Tax**
INDICTMENT or information—
Allegation as to value—
Of embezzled property. **Embez 29**
Of personal property. **Ind & Inf 104**
Of property stolen. **Rec S Goods 7(5)**
Bribe. **Brib 6(3)**
Variance between allegations and proof.
Ind & Inf 181
INSURANCE—
Avoidance for misrepresentation,
breach of warranty or condition.
Insurance 281
Forfeiture for breach of warranty, see
this index **Forfeitures**
Limitation of liability as to value or
property destroyed. **Insurance
498–500**
Marine insurance. **Insurance 473–475**
Part of value. **Insurance 501**
INTERNAL Revenue, see this index **Inter-
nal Revenue**
INTOXICATING liquors, recovery. **Int
Liq 328**
JUDICIAL notice—
Crim Law 304(19)
Evid 18
JURISDICTION affected by amount or
value in controversy, see this index
Jurisdictional Amount
LACHES affected by change of value.
Equity 72(4)
LAND sold under contract, see this index
Vendor and Purchaser
LAND taken for public use, see this index
Eminent Domain
MECHANICS' liens—
Evidence in proceeding to enforce lien.
Mech Liens 280(2)
Limitation of amount of lien to reason-
able value of labor or materials.
Mech Liens 161(3)
Right to lien affected by. **Mech Liens
54**
OPINION evidence, see this index **Opin-
ion Evidence**
PLEADING and proof as to value. **Dam-
ag 159(8)**
PRINCIPAL and agent, notice to agent of
facts affecting value. **Princ & A
177(4)**
PUBLIC service companies, regulation of
charges by commission. **Pub Ut 124,
126**
RENT, see this index **Rent**
REPLEVINED property—
Affidavit. **Replev 30**
Allegation of value in pleading. **Replev
59**
Depreciation in value as element of
damages. **Replev 78**
Judgment for value. **Replev 103, 106**
Verdict and findings. **Replev 96**
Writ of replevin. **Replev 37**
ROBBERY, see this index **Robbery**
SALES, see this index **Sales**
SERVICES, see this index **Services**
SLANDER of. **Libel 133**

VALUE—Cont'd
STOLEN property—
Burg 41(7)
Larc 6, 31, 46, 59, 72, 83
Rec S Goods 2, 7(5)
TAXATION—
According to value. **Tax 49**
Tax shelter valuation. **Tax 348(2)**
Apartment house—
Under income-capitalization ap-
proach. **Tax 349(5)**
Exemption. **Tax 212**
"Fullest extent possible" standard. **Tax
348.1(1)**
Property of cooperative housing corpo-
ration. **Tax 348.1(1)**
Tenants' improvements taxable to own-
ers of shopping center. **Tax 79**
Whether rendered worthless by toxic
waste in soil—
Evidence. **Tax 485(3)**
TROVER and conversion, see this index
Trover and Conversion
WATCHES'—
Evidence of—
Price affixed to by seller. **Evid
113(1)**

VALUED POLICIES
MARINE insurance. **Insurance 475**
PROPERTY or title, extent of loss and
liability. **Insurance 500**

VAN
APPLICABILITY of statute relating to operation of vehicles with passengers
under age of five. **Autos 148**

VANDALISM
. See generally, this index **Malicious Mis-
chief**
INSTRUCTION on related offense of—
Failure to give—
In burglary prosecution. **Crim Law
795(1)**

VARIANCE
AIR pollution. **Health & E 25.6(7)**
ATTACHMENT, see this index **Attach-
ment**
AWARD of arbitrators to submission. **Ar-
bit 57–57.3**
CERTIFICATE or declaratory statement
of mining location or claim, variation
of description from ground marks.
Mines 21(2)
EMINENT domain, see this index **Emi-
nent Domain**
INDORSEMENTS and signatures. **Forg
34(3)**
INTERNAL Revenue, see this index **Inter-
nal Revenue**
ISSUES, proof and variance relating
thereto, see this index **Issues, Proof
and Variance**
JUDGMENT—
Amendment or correction. **Judgm 305**
Amount of recovery. **Judgm 256(6)**
Attorney's fee. **Judgm 256(7)**
Costs. **Judgm 256(7)**
Findings, conformity of judgment.
Judgm 256
Grounds of action or defense. **Judgm
250**
Interest. **Judgm 256(7)**

VARIANCE—Cont'd
JUDGMENT—Cont'd
Parties, conformity of judgment to ver-
dict and findings. **Judgm 256(5)**
Pleadings, default judgment. **Judgm
117**
Process, pleadings, proofs, verdict or
findings. **Judgm 246–258**
Referee's report. **Judgm 257**
Special verdict and finding. **Judgm
256(2)**
Surplusage in verdict or findings.
Judgm 256(3)
Verdict and finding. **Judgm 256**
MUNICIPAL improvements—
Notice or petition and ordinance and
order. **Mun Corp 304(12)**
Preliminary and final estimates. **Mun
Corp 462**
Preliminary resolution or estimate of
cost and ordinance and order.
Mun Corp 304(13)
NOTICE and claim for injury from defect
or obstruction in street and pleading
or proof. **Mun Corp 816(11)**
OFFER to buy and acceptance. **Sales
23(4)**
OFFER to sell and acceptance. **Sales
22(4)**
PLEADING—
Bill of particulars and pleading. **Plead
328**
Ground for objections to evidence.
Plead 429
Declaration and process. **Plead 74**
Ground for abatement. **Abate & R 31**
Implied and constructive contracts.
Impl & C C 83
Pleading and instrument annexed, filed,
or referred to. **Plead 312**
Statement and process. **Plead 74**
PLEADING and proof—
See this index **Issues, Proof and Vari-
ance**
Judgment, bar or estoppel, see this in-
dex **Conclusiveness of Judgments
and Decrees**
PUBLIC officers and employees—
Disciplinary proceedings—
Notice or charge. **Offic 72.13**
SIGN—
Area variance. **Zoning 503**
TAX deed and prior tax proceedings as to
description of property. **Tax 764(3)**
WATER pollution. **Health & E 25.7(16)**
ZONING, see this index **Zoning**

VARIANCES OR EXCEPTIONS
ZONING, see this index **Zoning**

"VASCAR" COMPUTER–RECORDER
PRESUMPTION of accuracy—
To speed reading taken by. **Crim Law
388**

VASCULAR INJURY
WORKERS' compensation, accidental injury. **Work Comp 588**

VASECTOMY
PHYSICIAN—
Duty to disclose to patient material
risks of complications. **Phys 15(8)**
PHYSICIAN'S negligence resulting in
birth of unwanted child, damages.
Phys 18.110

ILLUSTRATION #2

PHYSICIANS & SURGEONS ⟳18.110

domen after hysterectomy, order granting new trial based on inadequacy of damages was appropriate unless hospital and surgeon consented in writing to additur raising total amount of judgment to $125,000. West's Ann.C.C.P. § 657.—Id.

Cal.App. 1981. Award of $450,000 in special and general damages to patient whose physician unlawfully injected silicone into her breasts was not excessive where she adduced evidence of more than $25,000 in special damages and of disruption in her normal activities and family life.—Nelson v. Gaunt, 178 Cal.Rptr. 167, 125 C.A.3d 623.

Award of punitive damages of $1,500,000 to patient whose physician had unlawfully injected silicone into her breasts was within discretion of jury.—Id.

In patient's action against physician, trial court was not required to make inquiry into physician's wealth before punitive damages could be awarded. West's Ann.Civ.Code § 3294.—Id.

Colo.App. 1985. "Wrongful pregnancy" cases are those actions where parents of healthy child bring claim on their own behalf for monetary and emotional damages suffered as result of giving birth to unwanted child.—Continental Cas. Co. v. Empire Cas. Co., 713 P.2d 384.

"Wrongful birth" claims are brought by parents who claim that they would have avoided conception or terminated pregnancy had they been properly advised of risks of birth defects to potential child, seeking recovery for their expenses in caring for deformed child, and for their own pain and suffering.—Id.

"Wrongful life" actions, as opposed to "wrongful pregnancy" or "wrongful birth" actions, are suits brought by impaired child, rather than by parents, and child alleges that but for defendant doctor or health care providers' negligent advice to, or treatment of, the parents, child would not have been born, and essence of child's claim is that defendants wrongfully deprived parents of information which would have prevented child's birth.—Id.

In wrongful life action, defendant must owe plaintiff legal duty, defendant must breach that duty, and breach must be proximate cause of plaintiff's harm.—Id.

Relevant causal relationship in wrongful life cases is between defendant's negligence and subsequent birth of child, not between defendant's negligence and genetic impairment of child. —Id.

Action for wrongful life is proper claim for relief.—Id.

Right to recovery for tort of wrongful life was established in medical malpractice action where physician admitted negligence and it was uncontroverted that physician's negligence resulted in child's birth.—Id.

Conn. 1982. Defendant physician took plaintiff patient as he found her and would be liable to plaintiff for effect of injuries caused by him even though their effect might be more serious than in case of normal person.—Bruneau v. Quick, 447 A.2d 742, 187 Conn 617.

In patient's action for claimed podiatric malpractice arising out of certain operative procedures performed by physician on feet of plaintiff, in view of fact that plaintiff, who, at age of 58 and before surgery was best ice skater at her age and level in New England, could no longer skate or dance with her husband, would experience depression, and had some difficulty tolerating walking, verdict in amount of $61,000 was not excessive.—Id.

Conn. 1982. Permitting parents to recover ordinary child-rearing costs as an element of damages was proper in action which arose out of allegedly negligent sterilization procedure and in

which jury was instructed to reduce potentially recoverable child-rearing expenses by value of benefits conferred on parents by having and raising child.—Ochs v. Borrelli, 445 A.2d 883, 187 Conn. 253, 187 Conn. 253.

Award of $49,985 for medical expenses and pain and suffering endured by mother, who underwent negligent sterilization operation, who had anxiety throughout her pregnancy that baby would be deformed, was unable to eat or sleep, suffered ruptured vein, underwent a second sterilization procedure causing her four weeks of serious discomfort and underwent painful X-ray procedure to verify success of such sterilization procedure, was not excessive.—Id.

Conn. 1980. No cause of action existed on behalf of mother for physical, mental and emotional harm caused by witnessing death of her daughter which was alleged to be result of physicians' medical malpractice based on facts that mother witnessed the deterioration of her daughter's health and momentary stopping of her daughter's heart while being administered mouth-to-mouth resuscitation by her and that mother participated in decision to discontinue extraordinary life-support methods.—Amodio v. Cunningham, 438 A.2d 6, 182 Conn. 80.

Del.Super. 1984. Husband who sought damages for his wife's inability to have children, because her uterus was removed after being perforated during doctor's attempted removal of an intrauterine device, and for witnessing physical and emotional pain and suffering of his wife, sought elements of damages which were properly within concept of loss of consortium.—Lacy v. G.D. Searle & Co., 484 A.2d 527.

D.C.App. 1984. Mother who alleged that negligent performance of tubal cauterization proximately caused her to become pregnant and give birth to child was not entitled to recover cost of rearing her healthy but unplanned child. —Flowers v. District of Columbia, 478 A.2d 1073.

Fla. 1984. Statute which requires trial court to reduce jury verdict award in medical malpractice cases by amount of all collateral source payments available to plaintiff, which only addresses liquidated collateral source payments which have been paid, was inapplicable to unliquidated future damages. West's F.S.A. § 768.-50.—Florida Physician's Ins. Reciprocal v. Stanley, 452 So.2d 514.

Fla. 1984. For public policy reasons, rearing damages for the birth of a healthy child are not allowed.—Fassoulas v. Ramey, 450 So.2d 822.

As a matter of law, benefits to parents outweigh their economic loss in rearing and educating a healthy, normal child.—Id.

As a matter of law, ordinary rearing expenses for a defective child are not recoverable as damages in Florida.—Id.

Special upbringing costs associated with a deformed child are recoverable as damages in Florida.—Id.

Fla.App. 1 Dist. 1985. Wrongful Death Act [West's F.S.A. §§ 768.16–768.27], by eliminating claims for pain and suffering of a person injured by an act of medical malpractice where death results from such injuries, did not also eliminate claims for pain and suffering of injured person where death did not result from the medical malpractice; Act is not applicable except in actions where it is claimed that the death of a person was caused by the wrongful act, negligence, or default of another.—Williams v. Bay Hosp. Inc., 471 So.2d 626.

Fla.App. 3 Dist. 1985. Award of $2,150 in dental malpractice action was reasonable in light of evidence presented and patient's actual damages.—Gumper v. Bach, 474 So.2d 420.

Fla.App. 3 Dist. 1982. Parents of a child, who is born as result of negligent vasectomy, are not entitled in "wrongful birth" negligence suit to past and future damages for care and upbringing expenses of subject child as against tort-feasor physician unless child is born with substantial physical or mental defects, in which event parents are entitled to recover special medical and educational expenses, apart from normal rearing costs, associated with raising such child to majority.—Ramey v. Fassoulas, 414 So.2d 198, approved 450 So.2d 822.

Parents of child have cause of action sounding in negligence against physician for performing negligent vasectomy, sterilization, or abortion, or for otherwise performing negligent medical service, which results in birth of unwanted child.— Id.

Fla.App. 4 Dist. 1983. Compensatory damages award of 12.47 million dollars in medical malpractice case was neither excessive nor unreasonable inasmuch as plaintiff, who suffered irreversible brain damage after his air supply was interrupted due to a malfunctioning respirator, was condemned to a 40-year life expectancy as a half-blind, hopelessly bedridden, pain-racked incompetent who required nearly $200,000 worth of medical care each year.—Florida Medical Center, Inc. v. Von Stetina By and Through Von Stetina, 436 So.2d 1022, reversed Florida Patient's Compensation Fund v. Von Stetina, 474 So.2d 783.

Fla.App. 5 Dist. 1983. Medical malpractice plaintiff was not entitled to punitive damages because record contained no basis to conclude that emergency room physician or hospital acted with malice, gross negligence or fraud in allegedly failing to diagnose and treat patient's condition.—Curry v. Cape Canaveral Hosp., 426 So.2d 64.

Fla.App. 5 Dist. 1982. Where jury in medical malpractice case concluded that both surgeon and patient contributed in part to worsened condition of patient's arm, and compensatory damages were apportioned accordingly, jury's failure to award anything for pain and suffering present or future could not be sustained inasmuch as two surgeries must have caused some amount of pain and suffering which patient would not otherwise have experienced.—Ledbetter v. Todd, 418 So.2d 1116.

Fla.App. 5 Dist. 1982. A child born with physical or mental defects did not have a cause of action against anyone on account of having been born.—DiNatale v. Lieberman, 409 So.2d 512, appeal after remand Allen v. Hoover, 489 So.2d 1160.

If either parent can prove that child will require extraordinary care in future and that the negligence of the defendant caused, or will in the future cause, the parent to incur expenses for that extraordinary care, then the parent is entitled to recover damages in court for those extraordinary expenses.—Id.

Where there were allegations of negligence on part of physician or other health care provider and of extraordinary expenses which would be incurred for care of defective child, father had right to seek damages for negligent and wrongful birth of child.—Id.

Fla.App. 1981. There is no cause of action for wrongful life by illegitimate, for wrongful life by unwanted healthy baby or unwanted deformed child, born as result of failed sterilization or abortion, or for wrongful life by deformed child born as result of failure to diagnose and or inform his parents regarding inheritable disease. —Moores v. Lucas, 405 So.2d 1022.

Where woman wanted to become pregnant and bear child, and pregnancy and delivery in connection with her physically deformed son were no more difficult or painful than if son had been

ILLUSTRATION #3

Dr. John R. RAMEY and Manson, Kuckku and Middkiff, P. A., individually, and d/b/a Manson Clinic, Appellants,

v.

John FASSOULAS and Edith Fassoulas, individually and as husband and wife, Appellees.

No. 79–1573.

District Court of Appeal of Florida, Third District.

Feb. 23, 1982.

On Rehearing June 8, 1982.

Parents brought action against physician and his professional association based on medical malpractice for the two "wrongful births" of their children, one of whom was a normal child and the second of whom was substantially mentally and physically impaired. The Circuit Court, Dade County, Jack M. Turner, J., entered judgment on special verdict in favor of parents, and physician and professional association appealed. The District Court of Appeal, Hubbart, C. J., held that parents of a child, who is born as result of negligent vasectomy, are not entitled in "wrongful birth" negligence suit to past and future damages for care and upbringing expenses of subject child as against tort-feasor physician unless child is born with substantial physical or mental defects, in which event parents are entitled to recover special medical and educational expenses, apart from normal rearing costs, associated with raising such child to majority.

Reversed and remanded with directions.

Hendry, J., filed dissenting opinion.

1. Physicians and Surgeons ⟜18.110

Parents of a child, who is born as result of negligent vasectomy, are not entitled in "wrongful birth" negligence suit to past and future damages for care and upbringing expenses of subject child as against tort-feasor physician unless child is born with substantial physical or mental defects, in which event parents are entitled to recover special medical and educational expenses, apart from normal rearing costs, associated with raising such child to majority.

2. Physicians and Surgeons ⟜18.110

Parents of child have cause of action sounding in negligence against physician for performing negligent vasectomy, sterilization, or abortion, or for otherwise performing negligent medical service, which results in birth of unwanted child.

Wicker, Smith, Blomqvist, Davant, Tutan, O'Hara & McCoy and Richard A. Sherman, Miami, for appellants.

Horton, Perse & Ginsberg and Arnold R. Ginsberg, Hawkesworth & Schmick, Miami, for appellees.

Before HUBBART, C. J., HENDRY, J., and PEARSON, TILLMAN (Ret.), Associate Judge.

HUBBART, Chief Judge.

[1] The central issue presented for review by this appeal is whether the parents of a child, who is born as a result of a negligent vasectomy, are entitled in a "wrongful birth" negligence suit to past and future damages for the care and upbringing expenses of the subject child as against the tortfeasor physician who negligently performed the vasectomy. We hold that the parents are not entitled to damages for such past and future rearing expenses—unless the child is born with substantial physical or mental defects, in which event, the parents are entitled to recover the special medical and educational expenses, apart from the normal rearing costs, associated with raising such a child to majority, age 18. We, accordingly, reverse the final judgment entered below and remand for a new trial for failure of the trial court to strike, at least in part, the claim for past and future rearing expenses as to the children born in the instant case.

ILLUSTRATION #4

NEW YORK SUPPLEMENT, 2d SERIES

Vol. 301

511P2d32 Ind 441NE487 Md 417A2d461 430A2d607 Mass 496NE831 Wash 516P2d216 524P2d901 739P2d654 47NYL26 71A2d82s 13A2d696n 13A2d737n —519— (24NY569) (249NE394) s290NYS2d [762 302NYS2d [131 f304NYS2d1 [340 d313NYS2d1 [457 e313NYS2d1 [470 d314NYS2d1 [271 314NYS2d [457 316NYS2d1 [392 d319NYS2d [935 e319NYS2d1 [953 j319NYS2d [959 320NYS2d1 [270 f322NYS2d1 [868 j322NYS2d1 [870 323NYS2d [766 324NYS2d1 [48 j324NYS2d1 [52 f325NYS2d1 [197 333NYS2d [785 d335NYS2d2 [67 335NYS2d1 j335NYS2d1 [73 336NYS2d1 [78 338NYS2d [527 342NYS2d1 [160 349NYS2d1 [557 355NYS2d1 [746 361NYS2d1 [607	370NYS2d1 [579 j370NYS2d1 [582 372NYS2d1 [113 379NYS2d1 [654 d384NYS2d1 [482 396NYS2d [973 406NYS2d [629 f416NYS2d [987 425NYS2d1 [216 430NYS2d1 [832 437NYS2d1 [866 445NYS2d1 [474 472NYS2d1 [800 489NYS2d1 [423 489NYS2d [805 491NYS2d1 [95 491NYS2d2 [96 j491NYS2d [102 506NYS2d91 517NYS2d1 [305 520NYS2d [480 449US1315 66LE1532 101SC1641 Cir. 2 f445F2d11274 f445F2d21275 d447F2d1179 j447F2d1185 475F2d2442 475F2d448 529F2d11138 572F2d184 e579F2d1205 730F2d2847 730F2d1849 315FS1304 335FS1333 335FS11111 342FS1247 348FS1208 371FS1444 422FS1853 465FS1640 475FS1294 482FS1634 495FS1520 557FS1578 569FS1442 606FS609 622FS2247 625FS1758 f650FS153 652FS11065 658FS1200 671FS1217	54FRD1180 57FRD1167 40BRW2392 Cir. 3 481F2d1266 508F2d132 366FS11201 e398FS1134 443FS11101 53FRD1410 Cir. 4 j464F2d190 759F2d11179 Cir. 7 e644F2d1629 Cir. 9 83FRD1582 Ariz 604P2d1157 Iowa 185NW232 La 236So2d225 Me 265A2d616 N H 290A2d628 N J 258A2d375 263A2d131 N M 553P2d1289 Ohio 267NE407 Pa 267A2d856 267A2d858 470A2d1361 R I 306A2d813 S D 194NW169 583SW316 Tex 571P2d590 36BR15 37BR336 21Buf315 57Cor316 60Cor942 62Cor136 71CR560 71CR1424 72CR270 72CR299 73CR63 77CR249 81CR972 83CR844 85CR1606 38FR111 54FR171 1Hof116 1Hof126 1Hof163 1Hof180 4Hof620 5Hof32 7Hof825 7Hof844 10Hof114 10Hof161 10Hof1003 10Hof1052 53NYL85	21SR407 22SR373 23SR446 24SR61 30SR473 31SR104 45StJ65 47StJ74 60CaL14 25CLA199 26CLA457 41LCP(2)19 41LCP(2)35 41LCP(2)148 61MnL474 66MnL339 70NwL624 74NwL782 75NwL377 118PaL235 130PaL1127 27StnL775 28StnL726 49TxL217 49TxL236 65VaL1063 AL§11.03 95A2d12s 62A31078n —544— (24NY598) (249NE412) D400US548 D27LE596 D91SC520 s291NYS2d [881 s397US933 s25LE114 s90SC957 o307NYS2d1 [38 307NYS2d2 [38 e311NYS2d1 [139 j314NYS2d1 [940 q321NYS2d [582 q322NYS2d1 [358 q352NYS2d1 [711 383NYS2d6 385NYS2d1 [690 385NYS2d3 [691 401NYS2d1 [983 q408NYS2d1 [904 e432NYS2d [140 440NYS2d2 [937 j453NYS2d [929 535NYS2d [902 459US1276 74LE1452 103SC1623 Cir. 2	426F2d3627 398FS1129 Cir. 3 j449F2d148 Md 288A2d608 38BR329 21SR766 22SR108 45StJ431 56TxL804 13A21439s 38A2225s —554— (24NY609) (249NE419) s284NYS2d [997 s291NYS2d [227 j313NYS2d1 [488 313NYS2d1 [503 313NYS2d1 [852 324NYS2d1 [224 325NYS2d2 [268 326NYS2d1 [935 326NYS2d1 [198 326NYS2d1 [886 329NYS2d1 [713 f331NYS2d1 [484 f331NYS2d2 [484 338NYS2d1 [365 342NYS2d1 [367 349NYS2d [791 350NYS2d [480 352NYS2d1 [646 f354NYS2d2 [110 f355NYS2d2 [32 f355NYS2d2 [726 j355NYS2d2 [198 j355NYS2d [204 j355NYS2d [446 f355NYS2d1 [922 363NYS2d2 [572 366NYS2d1 [212 d369NYS2d2 [642 j369NYS2d2 [643 d372NYS2d1 [641 f378NYS2d1 [187 f378NYS2d2 [187	378NYS2d2 [952 f381NYS2d1 [340 f381NYS2d2 [340 d383NYS2d1 [329 d383NYS2d2 [329 j383NYS2d1 [332 j383NYS2d2 [332 f385NYS2d1 [958 385NYS2d1 [959 385NYS2d [973 f386NYS2d1 [461 f386NYS2d2 [461 j386NYS2d1 [503 j386NYS2d2 [465 391NYS2d [466 394NYS2d1 [968 d394NYS2d1 [935 d394NYS2d2 [935 j394NYS2d1 [818 396NYS2d [819 397NYS2d1 [648 397NYS2d1 [365 j397NYS2d1 [362 397NYS2d1 [367 400NYS2d [791 400NYS2d1 [112 400NYS2d1 [113 410NYS2d2 [636 412NYS2d1 [110 412NYS2d2 [724 412NYS2d2 [726 413NYS2d [904 j413NYS2d [905 d422NYS2d2 [681 f422NYS2d [922 d422NYS2d1 [683 d422NYS2d1 [683 d425NYS2d2 [245 f433NYS2d1 [255 f434NYS2d1 [402 f434NYS2d1 [437 f434NYS2d2 [522 f434NYS2d2 [522 j434NYS2d [523	d435NYS2d2 [309 435NYS2d1 [310 f435NYS2d [1008 j436NYS2d [872 e445NYS2d -[110 j445NYS2d [111 e445NYS2d1 [112 445NYS2d [191 445NYS2d2 [192 f446NYS2d1 [457 f446NYS2d2 [457 448NYS2d1 [832 450NYS2d [864 j451NYS2d [531 451NYS2d2 [531 454NYS2d2 [751 458NYS2d34 459NYS2d1 [818 459NYS2d2 [819 461NYS2d2 [108 j461NYS2d [243 e462NYS2d1 [423 j462NYS2d [426 463NYS2d [957 d467NYS2d1 [636 j467NYS2d [639 469NYS2d1 [33 j469NYS2d [954 h473NYS2d [360 j473NYS2d [364 j473NYS2d [370 474NYS2d1 [78 f474NYS2d1 [889 476NYS2d2 [305 e476NYS2d [306 q477NYS2d1 [437 478NYS2d1 [522 j478NYS2d [842	479NYS2d1 [476 480NYS2d1 [457 487NYS2d1 [702 488NYS2d1 [443 492NYS2d [557 493NYS2d1 [416 j493NYS2d [1016 498NYS2d2 [261 498NYS2d1 [705 498NYS2d2 [705 499NYS2d1 [168 501NYS2d1 [323 504NYS2d [694 508NYS2d1 [205 d510NYS2d2 [898 f513NYS2d [358 514NYS2d [409 515NYS2d1 [282 518NYS2d [614 d518NYS2d2 [956 523NYS2d [760 d525NYS2d2 [103 525NYS2d [214 j526NYS2d [834 533NYS2d2 [230 535NYS2d [373 Cir. 1 518F2d277 d354FS2814 Cir. 2 e724F2d119 353FS230 554FS1312 554FS2312 Cir. 4 489F2d1071 390FS871 Cir. 8 480F2d1467 347FS2667 572FS21202 Cir. 9 307FS1417 307FS2417 Cir. 10 e403FS1674 e403FS2674 Ariz *Continued*

Chapter IV

WRITING THE BRIEF

A. INTRODUCTION

1. The Purpose of the Brief. A brief systematically presents the arguments, authorities and relevant background material of a legal controversy and aids an appellate court in rendering a decision. Because of the large number of cases heard by each court, judges today often rely on briefs as the foundation of their decision-making process. A brief gives each party an equal opportunity to describe their position clearly, accurately, and assertively to the appellate court.

As an instrument of persuasion, the brief must be simple and interesting, with a compelling factual and legal foundation. Because the brief often serves as the court's resource for writing the opinion, the document must be complete and reliable. Strong advocacy requires the briefwriter to craft a fair and persuasive piece of writing that will lead the court to the writer's point of view rather than bombard it with conclusory statements.

2. Stylistic Guidelines. The writing skills you learned elsewhere apply equally well to legal writing. Those who enjoy writing in general may be surprised to learn that they enjoy writing briefs. The same challenges of imagination, phrasing, and structure must be met to yield a successful product. The general principles of prose writing that helped you turn out cogent collegiate papers should not be abandoned at the law school's door.

Keep in mind, however, that a brief is a persuasive piece of writing and you should gear each element of it should be geared toward convincing the court of the correctness of your position. You will want to present a core theory, and develop one or more lines of argument. Throughout the brief you are trying to tell a story which puts your client in the most favorable light possible.

3. Comparing Briefwriting and Oral Advocacy. The brief and the oral argument each have strengths and weaknesses as tools of persuasion and as means of conveying information. For example, numbers and dates are better absorbed visually than aurally and should therefore be emphasized in the brief. Also, the brief is the appropriate place to cite authority; citations flow more smoothly off the pen than off the tongue. Only through oral argument, however, can you sense the reactions of your audience and adjust your presentation to meet their concerns. Your brief should contain all of the information necessary for the court to reach a decision, while the oral argument gives you a chance to have a conversation with the court and to rebut arguments that your opponent raised in her brief that you did not deal with in yours.　A good brief, however will have anticipated the other side's arguments and dealt with them in the brief.　Devise your appellate game plan by recognizing the strategic values of the brief and the oral argument and exploiting the strengths of each.

A brief should be simple, organized, interesting, complete, and reliable.　Within those constraints, you have considerable discretion in selecting what writing style to use.　Opinions differ as to what tone is ultimately the most persuasive.　Many advocates adhere to a dispassionate, scholarly approach, relying heavily on authorities.　Others prefer an aggressively adversarial tack, constantly going for "the jugular," building drama and emotion, and decimating the assertions of the other side.　Still others strike a balance between these extremes.

Some basic principles should be applied,

- Strategically select every word by analyzing its tactical and literary value.　Be careful, for example, when choosing the names for the parties in your case.　The overuse of "appellant" and "appellee" in a brief can be confusing to a reader who does not share your intimate understanding of the record.　Instead, characterize the parties in a manner that will influence the reader's perception of them.　A brief adopting a formalistic approach should be formal in naming the parties (e.g., "Parent," "Doctor").　A brief appealing to the court's sense of equity would probably use more personal titles (e.g., "the Bell-Wesleys," "Dr. O'Toole").　Another device is to try to evoke the reader's empathy for your client by referring to him with a personal title and using a more formal title for his adversary.　Regardless of which route you select, remember to be consistent throughout your brief.

- Realize the potential of various parts of speech for conveying emphasis.　A forceful argument will contain action verbs, rather than only forms of the verb "to be."　"Spot bit Jane" describes the scenario more dramatically than does the passive construction "Jane was bitten by Spot."　However, when presenting damaging facts and arguments you can subtly downplay their force by using the passive voice.

- Do not rely on complex, pompous language.　Legalese is not inherently persuasive and should not be used except in exceptional circumstances.　Simplify your language.　Your eloquence will not suffer and you will enhance the force of your arguments.　For example, multiple subordinate clauses may tend to confuse rather than persuade the reader.

- Avoid using extended quotations.　Short quotations can be used to add variation or emphasis to your argument.　If there is no concise quotation, a paraphrase with a citation may better demonstrate how an author that you have researched aids your position. An impatient reader is likely to skip over a lengthy quotation. Explain the relevance of the quotation yourself, rather than expecting the court to figure out how it applies to your case.

B. PARTS OF THE BRIEF

A comprehensive brief consists of various parts, each designed to convey a specific type of information. The parts are as follows:

1.   the questions presented

2.   the facts

3.   the arguments supporting your position

4.   conclusion

Each component has a separate but complementary purpose so that the whole can function as a persuasive instrument.

1. Questions Presented. First, the brief must set the agenda for the court by presenting what questions should be answered in order to decide the case. A judge's initial reaction to the seriousness and merit of the appeal is often based upon this indication of what the counsel considers to be vital to his case. Like the brief as a whole, the questions themselves must be simple, interesting, complete, and reliable.

Crafting the questions presented is a useful exercise with which to begin writing your brief because it forces you to frame and clarify the key issues raised by the facts and rulings below. Some people, however, prefer to save this task for last, after they have articulated their argument in detail. Either way, plan to spend a lot of time writing and rewriting the questions. They create the first impression of your version of the issues for the judge. Don't waste this initial opportunity for advocacy.

a. How many? As you create your core theory you should give some thought to the number of questions presented. In making this decision, determine how many winning arguments are on your side. The number of questions you present will correspond to the arguments you decide to make. Avoid weakening your strong points by associating them with less momentous arguments. These considerations, in conjunction with space restrictions, will probably leave you with two, three, or to really push it, four arguments in your brief.

b. Structure. The questions presented are a substructural requirement usually placed at the beginning of the text. Present them in the order in which their corresponding arguments will appear in the brief. Each question should be independent and require no reference to any point contained in a previous one. (For example, do not write, "Is *such action* prohibited by the Establishment Clause?") Although your argument may be complex, try to craft clear and easy-to-read questions. Questions with many subclauses tend to get convoluted.

c. Substance. Your questions should suggest an answer that you want the court to reach. To achieve this end, questions should incorporate important facts of your case and the law you wish the court to apply. This enables you to impart some of the flavor of your argument to the reader from the moment he picks up the brief. Fact-filled questions are almost always more useful than formless, abstract questions of law. Your questions presented should serve as signposts for your arguments and indicate which side you are arguing. They should plant the first seeds of persuasion.

When formulating your questions, avoid the easy mistake of assuming the very issue that is in dispute. For example, the question "Does an unreasonable search violate the Fourth Amendment," assumes that the search was unreasonable. This question is poorly crafted because the real issue is whether the particular search in the case was an unreasonable search. There is no question that if the search was unreasonable, it would violate the Fourth Amendment.

You want to suggest with your questions that given this particular problem, the court can reasonably rule only one way. You should be careful not to irritate with overly biased questions that suggest by their stridency the inevitable counter-argument. Questions presented should be answerable by either a yes or a no. For purpose of symmetry, some people try to frame all of the questions in a given brief so that they are answered the same way, either all "yes" or all "no," in support of their position.

d. Examples. Different advocates arguing *Bell-Wesley v. O'Toole* might draft the following questions presented:

Not far enough:

Is a doctor who negligently performs a vasectomy liable for the costs of raising a child when the husband subsequently impregnates his wife and they have an unplanned baby?

Too far:

Where a couple, after having several congenitally deformed children who died soon after birth, has a child conceived after an unsuccessfully performed vasectomy, and refused to abort, or give the child up for adoption, should the doctor who performed the vasectomy be held liable for all the costs of raising that child when the couple could well afford to have the child, and benefited from the doctor's negligence by receiving the healthy child that they had always wanted?

More appropriate:

Should a doctor whose negligent performance of a sterilization inflicted numerous injuries upon a couple be held responsible for the full extent of his negligence by requiring him to compensate the couple for the medical costs, the physical and emotional pain and suffering, and the extensive financial costs associated with raising a child?

2.   The Introduction.   Use of an introduction in the brief has become more common in recent years.   A one-paragraph road map of the essential facts and the course of the advocate's arguments is often quite useful to judges, particularly in complex cases.   The introduction should be clear, concise, and devoid of citations.   Rules governing the permissible location of an introduction vary by jurisdiction.

3.   The Statement of Facts.   The Statement of Facts, sometimes called the Statement of the Case, tells your client's view as to what happened in the "real world" to bring this case into court.   Both sides must present a complete and reliable, yet simple and interesting, version of the facts of the case.   Those facts are the material from which you draw your arguments, but they are also the place where you can win or lose your case.   After reading your Statement of Facts, the judge should want to interpret the law in your favor.

a.   Identifying the facts.   Facts can be divided into two categories—substantive and procedural.   Substantive facts are concerned with events that happened before the litigation and at trial.   Procedural facts describe the legal path that the case has taken up to the point of your brief.   In complex cases, advocates may present these two types of facts separately.   For example, they might title this section of their brief, "Statement of the Case," and under this section have two subheadings entitled, "Proceedings Below" and "Statement of Facts."   Others combine both types of facts in a general statement of the case.   Regardless of how substantive and procedural facts are organized, both must be included.

b.   Choosing the facts.   You must sort out the relevant facts from the irrelevant ones contained in the record.   The decision as to what is relevant is often a commonsense one.   Normally, any fact actually used to support either side's position will be relevant.

You should be sure to include all the important facts supporting your position.   As for the facts relating to your opponent's position, omission of the most relevant facts on the other side is likely to impair your credibility.   A good Statement of the Facts will do more than just summarize the record, it will shape the facts into a narrative which is interesting and favorable to your position.

c. Sticking to the record. You must, as a general rule, use only the facts presented in the "four corners" of the record. However, there are limited exceptions. You can draw inferences from facts in the record. You can use facts subject to "judicial notice." Use admissions of the other side as positive proof of a fact that you wish to establish.

The creativity that you demonstrate in presenting a persuasive fact situation must not, under any circumstances, extend to making up or exaggerating information. A judge will not let a fabricated fact slide by as a clever inference. An appellate court must rely on the record. All assumptions of fact must be firmly grounded in the record. Certain undeniable assertions, however, such as the fact that apples do not fall up, can be introduced without appearing in the record. Other information, like the conclusions of relevant sociological studies, can be used even though they are not part of the record as long as proper authority is cited. (For examples of citations to the record, see the Statements of Facts in both briefs in *Bell-Wesley v. O'Toole*.)

Remember when doing your research that you are researching the potential legal arguments that can be used to support your position. You cannot, as an appellate attorney, research new evidence, or make it up.

However, holes in the record are not necessarily useless. You can successfully use "negative facts" to buttress your position. Negative facts are facts that the other side can neither establish nor disprove because of holes in the record. The advocate can effectively use negative facts to create a gap of essential knowledge, requiring a ruling in her client's favor. For example, a defendant-appellee may show that the plaintiff-appellant never met his burden of proof by pointing to the absence in the record of facts indicating otherwise. Or the advocate can fill a hole with hypotheticals, each as likely as the next, all designed to demonstrate the invalidity of her opponent's position given this lack of vital information. For example, the *Bell-Wesley v. O'Toole* record is silent on the issue of whether Scott and Rebecca ever considered adopting a child after learning that there was a high likelihood that any child they conceived would suffer a congential birth defect. Nonetheless, in the appellants' statement of the case, one sentence makes an inference that: "[a]lthough they could have adopted a child, they instead chose to devote their time and energy to their careers and each other." (See p. 67.) Do not be afraid to make effective use of holes in the record: holes have won many cases for clever appellate attorneys.

d. Organizing the facts. The organization of the facts also serves to further the goals of the brief. Every word in the statement of facts should be geared toward making the brief a better instrument of persuasion or a more complete and reliable resource. A good starting point in writing the Statement of Facts is to think about which facts are strongest for your side, and how you can highlight those facts.

A chronological narrative may or may not be the most persuasive structure for telling your story. "This happened, then that happened" probably lends an air of routineness to the activities depicted, which may or may not be the image you wish to convey. Consider starting with the conflict or the injury, if appropriate. Never forget to consider the impact of the specific words that you choose. Use active verbs for your strong points. Use labels that will appropriately characterize the parties. Attempt to use words which carry effective connotations. Make sure, also, to take it from square one. Introduce the characters and spell out abbreviations. Do not let your statement of the facts leave the court with needless questions.

e. Handling adverse facts. Reliability is essential. Glaring omissions of adverse facts central to the other side's case will decrease your credibility with the court. The negative side of the case will appear less damaging if you cautiously disclose it first.

There are ways of downplaying the dangerous, of course. Passive verbs can dilute the force of statements. The damaging material can be placed in a subordinate clause. Also, once you have mentioned the harmful fact, there is no need to emphasize it. For example, while an appellant needs to disclose that there was an adverse judgment below, she need not disclose that the district judge rejected each and every contention. Rest assured that the appellee will mention that. For example, in the *Bell-Wesley v. O'Toole* briefs, the doctor's attorney referred to his client's negligence by saying Dr. O'Toole "performed a vasectomy" and "mistakenly informed" Mr. Bell-Wesley that he was sterile. (See p. 88) On the other hand, the Bell-Wesleys' attorney characterized the same acts as "repeated acts of negligence" in performing both the vasectomy and the sperm count. (See p. 68.)

f. Separating fact from argument. Your desire to paint a persuasive factual picture must not cross the boundary into argument. You risk invoking the court's ire and losing credibility if you markedly slant the facts. Let the facts tell the story themselves. They are used to support your conclusions; they must not be expressed as conclusions. For example, you can emphasize the defendant's obviously improvident actions, but you should not label them as negligent unless you also remind the court that the plaintiff charged the defendant with negligence. In making arguments substantiated by holes in the record, for example, mention the holes in your Statement of the Facts, but explain the significance of the lack of information in the argument section of the brief. It is up to the court to draw the legal conclusion once you have persuasively pointed it out.

4. The Arguments. The arguments comprise the body of the brief. By this point, you have chosen the arguments after considering the legal precedent, policy, and facts of your case. You have tossed out weaker or less clear ones because including them might dilute the force of your main points. You have buttressed your ideas with the necessary authority. You have anticipated, preempted, or rebutted your opponent's crucial arguments and have distinguished his key cases. Now the only thing left to do is write.

a. Argument headings. Each argument begins with an argument heading, in capital letters, single spaced. Each heading should identify a specific portion of the argument to be advanced in that section of the brief. The headings should be complete sentences.

The argument headings should state affirmatively the resolution of the issues raised in the questions presented. An effective argument heading will clue the reader in to the applicable law, to the way in which the law applies to the facts of the case, and to the conclusion that follows from that application. However, do not try to fit every relevant legal or factual issue into the heading. Aim for a concise statement of the essence of your argument. Be careful with your use of strong adjectives and adverbs which might exaggerate your argument.

b. Subheadings. Subheadings can be used to summarize and partition arguments. They are typed in lower case, with initial capitals, and are underscored. When an argument is relatively simple, as in many moot court briefs, keep in mind that subheadings might interrupt the general flow of the argument.

c. Organization and structure of arguments. In organizing your brief, phrase your arguments in the affirmative and put the strongest ones first.

The introductory paragraph of each argument should make clear which issue you are about to argue. The issue should be framed as a legal issue which you are presenting to the court for resolution. You should then narrow the legal issue to the particulars of your case. A good general format for each argument is the pattern of a logical syllogism. Your argument would then look something like this:

- Introductory statement of the legal standard, framed in terms of this case;

- Application of the legal standard to the facts of the case;

- Summary;

- Rebuttal of opponent's assertion on this point. This formula is not set in stone. For example, depending on the circumstances you might choose first to rebut your opponent's assertions and then end with the main thrust of your argument.

An effective approach to organization is to make the first sentence of each paragraph a topic that tells the reader what will be discussed in that paragraph. A good test of the logical structure and cohesiveness of your brief is to read the first sentence of each paragraph. If this scan gives you a complete idea of the facts of your case and of the legal reasoning that you are using, then you are on the right track. If it doesn't, then it is time to reorganize and rewrite.

d. Substance of the argument. Your argument should not be comprised of unsupported assertions that simply tell the court it should rule in your favor. Rather, you must provide the cases, the precedent, and the authorities that will give the court the tools to reach that decision.

As you write your argument, identify the key elements of the cases you have researched that are favorable to you. Tie those elements into the facts of your case. If a favorable case is particularly similar to yours, you may want to discuss that case at greater length in your brief by specifically explaining its relevance and value.

If you are advocating for a change or a modification in the law as it has developed in the cases, be sure to include references to any legal scholars or other authorities who have also argued for such a change. Remember it is your job to make the court feel "comfortable" with accepting your arguments. While your own arguments based on public policy, for example, are necessary, an argument studded with authority will help prove to the court that the need for a change in the law has been considered elsewhere and is now appropriate.

The procedural posture of your case can also be very helpful to you as you develop your arguments. If the lower courts ruled in your favor, you may want to emphasize that point. The court may like the status quo and therefore might be inclined to affirm the decision below.

e. Rebuttal and preemption of arguments. Your argument should embrace and respond to your opponent's arguments. Evading or concealing the difficult points will leave the resolution of these points to the court without any guidance from you. The tone of each brief must remain affirmative and not convey a totally defensive posture. You can approach rebuttal either by addressing the other side's arguments as part of the affirmative presentation of your own thesis, or you can attack each of your opponent's arguments by directly confronting them. Careful drafting of the rebuttal to your opponent's arguments will help reinforce your core theory and keep the judge from agreeing too readily with your adversary. Never rely solely on conclusory statements characterizing your opponent's position as dead wrong, because she will probably have mounted a relatively convincing case and your blanket dismissal will only detract from your own credibility. Instead, try to show the illogic of the argument, to demonstrate how the facts fail to support the legal conclusion, and to point out the unfortunate consequences that would flow from a decision for your opponent. Criticize the authority used as unpersuasive or off point. But remember, attack the argument, not your opponent.

Most moot court programs use a staggered exchange system that resembles that of most appellate courts. The appellant files her brief first, then the appellee files his brief in response. Occasionally the appellant has the option of filing a second, shorter brief in reply to the appellee.

The appellee, because of his position as respondent, will spend more time rebutting and will have the advantage of knowing exactly what to rebut because he will have seen his opponent's brief. Appellant does not have this opportunity to highlight weaknesses in her adversary's brief unless she does so in the reply brief, or in oral argument, and should plan accordingly. The appellant, however, has the advantage of making the initial impression on the court.

Due to the limited time between the filing of the appellant's brief and the due date for the appellee's response, the appellee must do most of his research and outline his arguments before he receives his opponent's brief. When it comes to writing, a point-by-point refutation is rarely the ideal format for an appellee's brief. Arguments independent of those raised by the appellant are often stronger and more persuasive.

f. Arguing in the alternative. For some legal arguments you will find during the course of research that there are fall back positions. If the court fails to agree with your main position, you have a contingent position on which they can still rule in your favor. For example, you might argue in *Bell-Wesley* that based on the law and facts Dr. O'Toole was not negligent in performing the vasectomy. In the alternative, you might argue the following: Alternatively, even if Dr. O'Toole is negligent, he should not be required to compensate the Bell-Wesleys because they nonetheless desired a healthy child. The concern with arguing in the alternative is that you undermine the force of your main argument.

5. The Conclusion. The brief should end with a section entitled, "Conclusion," in which you state the remedy (or relief) you want the court to order. Your conclusion should not contain any new information. Also, resist the attempt to summarize your arguments. Summaries can be harmful because it is impossible to know which components of your arguments a court will find persuasive. Rather than risk summarizing in a way the court will find unpersuasive, leave the court to ponder the fully developed arguments in your arguments section. Also, page limits will require leaving out some details, and it is better to leave out a recapitulation of arguments than a useful authority or extra paragraph of legal argument.

C. USE OF AUTHORITY

Authorities are not glorified punctuation marks that must appear at the conclusion of every sentence in a brief. Rather, when properly used, they aid in convincing the reader to adopt the propositions you asserted. Courts operate on the principle of stare decisis, so judges appreciate your indentifying what prior judges have done.

When selecting authorities to use in a citation, choose the ones with the greatest relevance (generally referred to as being "on point") and the greatest weight, based on their sources. Since many moot court cases are set in mythical jurisdictions and are cases of first impression, opinions from the Supreme Court of the United States, a federal circuit court, or a state court of last resort are the most persuasive sources. You may also cite a variety of jurisdictions to indicate that a given proposition is widely accepted. In this situation, of course, three cases from three states will be more effective than three cases from one state.

Uncontested propositions of law, such as the definition of negligence, rarely require more than one authority in a citation. Nothing is to be gained from merely stringing citations together. Put in the authority that you need to achieve credibility and stop there.

1. Use of Parentheticals. In many instances the most effective way to use a case is to paraphrase the principle it stands for and follow that with a citation. However, judges are not familiar with most reported decisions, and they and their law clerks have neither the time nor the energy to read them all. Unless an authority supports only a general principle, an unelaborated or "bare" cite, giving only the case name and the reporter, will not help the court. Parentheticals, abstracting the facts of the case and/or quoting critical language, aid the reader by explaining the relevance, similarity, or difference of the cited case to the case at hand. Reading the footnotes in a hornbook will give you a feel for how to summarize cases in this way. (For examples of explanatory parentheticals, refer to the briefs in *Bell-Wesley v. O'Toole.*)

Cases that are particularly crucial to your argument, such as those propounding a rule that you seek to follow, may need more extensive treatment than a parenthetical. You may devote a small paragraph to explaining how the legal principle in that case governs the issue now before the court, or why it must be distinguished. Remember: in either situation, argue your own facts.

2. Contrary Authority. For the sake of reliability and completeness, important cases standing *against* the propositions advanced in the brief should be cited. You should distinguish these cases, if possible, either in text or in a parenthetical. When citing these cases, signal them with *"But see"* or *"Contra."* They will undoubtedly be cited by the opposition, and you may be able to reduce their impact by undermining their logic, or distinguishing them on their facts. Citation of contrary authority lets the court know that you have been thorough, and may help negate any damage done by the adverse cases.

D.　FORMALITIES

Now that you've done the hard work, you can preoccupy yourself with some technical details needed to make your brief look like a brief.

1.　Title Page. A title page provides the relevant information about the case: the court, the docket number, the names of the parties, the names of the attorneys, and the date and place of hearing.

A full designation of the parties (e.g., "Plaintiff-Appellant") should appear on the title page, but need not be repeated anywhere else in the brief. In most state jurisdictions and lower federal courts, the original order of the parties is maintained in the case on appeal. The Supreme Court of the United States names the appealing party first.

Counsels' names, formal title (e.g., "Attorney for the Appellee"), and the date and place of the oral argument are placed in the lower right hand corner.

2.　Table of Contents. The table of contents should list the components of the brief, including argument headings, subheadings, and the conclusion, along with the page number on which they can be found.

3.　Table of Citations. Here the writer lists all of the authorities used and indicates where they are cited in the brief. The table of citations demands great technical care and thus produces the most headaches and eyestrain in briefwriting. Citations must be accurate and complete, and must include all of the information required by *A Uniform System of Citation*. All page numbers, volume numbers, underlining, parentheses, brackets, and spacing should be checked carefully. Consult the tables of citations from the *Bell-Wesley v. O'Toole* briefs for examples of proper form for typewritten citations.

The list of citations may be divided into at least three sections: cases, statutes, and miscellaneous. Entries should be arranged alphabetically within each category. "Miscellaneous" can be subdivided into "Restatements," "Treatises," etc., if need be. Recheck your moot court rules to make sure that you have not exceeded the allowable number of cited authorities.

E.　PITFALLS TO AVOID:　FACT ANEMIA AND THE WHODUNIT SYNDROME

There are two frequently diagnosed syndromes encountered in many first attempts at appellate briefwriting. First is Fact Anemia. Rather than argue the facts of her case, the advocate producing a fact-anemic brief will devote long paragraphs to the historical evolution of a current legal standard. Extended quotations often accompany this affliction. Befuddled judges may glance at the cover page of the brief to make sure that they have not accidentally picked up a law review article.

This style is simply not persuasive. Direct references to the facts of the case are essential ingredients of your arguments. The court must apply principles of law to the particular facts of the case. You should attempt to incorporate facts into virtually every paragraph of the argument.

The second commonly observed syndrome is the whodunit. The writer gives clues, and the court, as if it were reading a murder mystery, must wait in suspense until reaching the conclusion. Many briefwriters seem reluctant, after weeks of scrupulous analysis and insights of intuition, to give away the punchline.

This is counterproductive. Stating the conclusion early and often is a must for a persuasive brief. Since the substance of many appellate cases is less compelling than the plots of most detective stories, you have to tell the reader why to keep reading. Otherwise, you may lose him on page five, long before he reaches your brilliantly crafted climax on page seven. In short, the destination of your argument should appear at the beginning. Tell the court what you are going to say, say it, and then conclude by summarizing what you have said. An inverse pyramid is much more persuasive than suspense.

F. SO YOU'RE OVER THE PAGE LIMIT, AND OTHER EDITING TIPS

Many have said that there is no good writing, only good rewriting. Whether or not you are indeed over the page limit, virtually any first draft of anything can use judicious editing.

1. Rewriting. There are two editing techniques that you may find useful. First, try the "What do you mean?" test. Reread your brief with an eye to convoluted paragraphs and sentences. Pause at these places; think about what you mean to say; and rewrite them in the form of a cogent explanation.

Second, avoid "slash and burn" editing by looking for certain patterns of words which can instinctively be crossed out wherever they appear, without any loss of meaning. Examples of such terms are: "It can be argued," "It seems that," "Cases have clearly held," and "It is beyond argument that." Just leave them out. Your prose will be that much clearer, stronger, and shorter.

2. Polishing. You can tighten your brief by eliminating string cites, summarizing lengthy quotations, putting subsidiary points in footnotes, and not devoting scarce space to arguing uncontroverted points of law. Polish your vocabulary. Eliminate unnecessary adverbs. Change passive constructions to active wherever you have not intentionally used the passive voice. Jettison the legalese.

Finally, editing gives you a good excuse to proofread. Judges are not going to decide cases based on animosity inspired by a misspelling. Uncorrected errors indicate that the brief, having not been read for those errors, may be equally unreliable in substance, reasoning, or its analysis of authorities. Do not let your credibility flounder because of an unnoticed typographical error.

G. SAMPLE BRIEFS: BELL–WESLEY v. O'TOOLE

Sample briefs for both parties in the case of *Bell-Wesley v. O'Toole* begin on the following page. The brief for the plaintiff-appellants, Rebecca and Scott Bell-Wesley, is intended to be rather strident in tone. The brief for the defendant-appellee, Dr. Stephen O'Toole, adopts a cooler, more reasoned style.

IN THE SUPREME COURT OF THE
STATE OF AMES

Civil Action No. 90-2004

SCOTT AND REBECCA BELL-WESLEY, Plaintiff-Appellants

v.

DR. STEPHEN O'TOOLE, Defendant-Appellee

BRIEF FOR THE PLAINTIFF-APPELLANTS

Jane E. Harvey
Attorney for the
Plaintiff-Appellants

Argument: March 22, 1991
Ames Courtroom
7:30 p.m.

TABLE OF CONTENTS

TABLE OF AUTHORITIES

MISCELLANEOUS

QUESTIONS PRESENTED

Should traditional tort principles be defied by denying recovery to parents who suffered serious injuries from a doctor's negligent performance of a vasectomy and of a sperm count resulting in the birth of an unplanned, unwanted child?

Should a doctor whose negligent performance of a sterilization and of a sperm count inflicted numerous injuries upon an innocent couple be held responsible for the full extent of his negligence, including the medical costs, the physical and emotional pain and suffering, and the extensive financial costs associated with the birth of a child?

STATEMENT OF THE CASE

Appellants Rebecca and Scott Bell-Wesley brought this civil action in the Superior Court for the State of Ames to recover for the injuries resulting from defendant Dr. Stephen O'Toole's negligence in the performance of a vasectomy and in subsequent testing and consultation. The injuries the Bell-Wesleys suffered are those associated with the unwanted conception and birth of their child, Frank Michael Bell. The Bell-Wesleys appeal the Superior Court's failure to recognize their wrongful birth claim.

1

Rebecca and Scott Bell-Wesley are established professionals who live in Holmes, Ames. Scott works as an architect in the Holmes City Planning Department. Rebecca, an attorney, accepted a position as First Assistant Attorney General of the State of Ames in 1981, shortly after her husband's vasectomy. (R.7)

Before January 1990, Rebecca Bell-Wesley gave birth to three congenitally deformed children, each of whom died in infancy. (R.1) Dr. O'Toole informed the Bell-Wesleys that there was a seventy-five percent probability that any child they conceived would suffer the same deformity. With this knowledge, Scott and Rebecca made a conscious decision to lead a childless life. (R.1) Although they could have adopted a child, they instead chose to devote their time and energy to their careers and each other. On October 16, 1988, the defendant performed a vasectomy on Scott Bell-Wesley to insure that the couple would remain childless permanently. (R.2) Three months later O'Toole performed a sperm count on Scott Bell-Wesley and informed him that the operation had rendered him sterile. (R.2)

In April 1989, Rebecca Bell-Wesley discovered that she was pregnant. The Bell-Wesleys refused to abort the child on moral grounds. (R.8) They also chose not to undergo amniocentesis. (R.6) On January 4, 1990, Rebecca Bell-Wesley gave birth to a healthy baby boy, Frank Michael Bell. (R.2) The Superior Court concluded as a matter of fact that the defendant's negligence

2

caused this birth; Dr. O'Toole failed to sever the tubes of Scott's vas deferens properly, and compounded his negligence by misperforming the sperm count. (R.10)

The Bell-Wesleys brought this medical malpractice action to recover the substantial injuries caused by O'Toole's carelessness. While Rebecca and Scott love Frank deeply, his conception and birth have nonetheless caused them severe emotional, physical, and financial harm. In addition to the pain and the substantial medical expenses related to the pregnancy, the Bell-Wesleys suffered considerable trauma from the conception and birth of a child whom they expected to be deformed. (R.2,3) Frank's birth has forced the Bell-Wesleys to alter their lives dramatically. (R.8) Both parents have lost, and will continue to lose, time and wages from their careers in order to care for the child. (R.7) After deciding to remain childless, Rebecca decided to devote more time to her career and accepted an important promotion with the Attorney General's office. Her salary increased from $31,000 to $47,000 per year. Rebecca's leave of absence in connection with the pregnancy has placed her job in jeopardy. (R.4) The financial and emotional costs of raising Frank present the Bell-Wesleys with a formidable burden.

While the Superior Court recognized O'Toole's repeated acts of negligence, it refused to recognize the Bell-Wesleys' claim for wrongful birth. Instead, the court limited the recovery to $10,000, covering only the medical costs, pain and suffering, and

3

loss of consortium immediately associated with the vasectomy.
The Bell-Wesleys appeal to this court for recognition of their
wrongful birth claim, seeking to recover for all the injuries
caused by defendant's negligence.

ARGUMENT

I.   THE BELL-WESLEYS' WRONGFUL BIRTH CLAIM MUST BE RECOGNIZED
     BECAUSE DR. O'TOOLE'S NEGLIGENT STERILIZATION OPERATION
     AND SPERM COUNT CAUSED THEM SUBSTANTIAL PHYSICAL,
     EMOTIONAL, AND FINANCIAL INJURY.

Basic common law tort principles mandate recognition of
the Bell-Wesleys' wrongful birth claim against Dr. O'Toole.
The couple's cause of action is based upon the elements which
constitute any negligence claim: duty, negligence, proximate
cause, and injury. See W. Prosser, Law of Torts § 30 (4th ed.
1971). As the trial court found, on two separate occasions Dr.
O'Toole breached a professional duty of care toward the
Bell-Wesleys. (R.8) O'Toole's negligent performance of Scott's
vasectomy and of the sperm count proximately caused the
conception and birth of the Bell-Wesleys' unplanned child.
(R.8) While the trial court denied that a healthy child's
birth could be accompanied by any injury to its parents, the
Bell-Wesleys have in fact met with serious physical, financial,
and emotional injuries. They have also suffered the violation
of their constitutionally protected right to self-determination
in the realm of family planning. The policies that underpin
every tort cause of action, deterring tortfeasors and
compensating their victims, compel recognition of the

Bell-Wesleys' wrongful birth claim. The Bell-Wesleys' claim is "indistinguishable from an ordinary medical malpractice action." <u>Sherlock v. Stillwater Clinic</u>, 260 N.W.2d 169, 174 (Minn. 1977) (failed vasectomy resulting in birth of healthy, unplanned child created cause of action against negligent physician, with damages allowed for pregnancy, birth, and childrearing). More than sixty state and federal cases have recognized wrongful birth claims. Note, <u>Wrongful Birth: A Child of Tort Comes of Age</u>, 50 U. Cin. L. Rev. 65 (1981).

For Rebecca and Scott, the trial court's antiquated notion that the birth of a child is always a "blessing" is meritless. Frank's conception and birth substantially injured the Bell-Wesleys' physical, emotional, and financial well-being. Rebecca's pregnancy was accompanied by the severe emotional trauma which, after the birth of three deformed children, the Bell-Wesleys sought to avoid through sterilization. Moreover, the couple's decision to undergo an irreversible sterilization operation demonstrated that they rejected traditional attitudes towards procreation. While they could have adopted children, Rebecca and Scott instead chose to pursue a childless lifestyle, recognizing that parenthood entails numerous costs, burdens, and responsibilities which may outweigh its attendant joys. Where a couple elects not to have children, it should be presumed that the birth of a child does not benefit them. <u>Hartke v. McKelway</u>, 707 F.2d 1544, 1552 (D.C. Cir. 1983) (failed tubal ligation, resulting in birth of healthy child, created wrongful birth claim against the physician), <u>cert. denied</u>, 104 S.Ct. 425 (1983). The Bell-Wesleys reassessed their opportunities and resources and radically altered their beliefs about the purposes and goals of their marriage. They decided to devote more time to each other and to their careers, only to have their expectations shattered as a result of O'Toole's repeated negligence.

Policy considerations dictate that these injuries to Scott and Rebecca be compensated like those in any other medical malpractice action. The general sentiment of the American public today is one of respect for family planning decisions. Tens of millions employ contraceptives daily to prevent the birth of children; these persons, "by their conduct, express the sense of the community." <u>Troppi v. Scarf</u>, 31 Mich. App. 240, 253, 187 N.W.2d 511, 517 (1971) (negligent filling of a birth control prescription with tranquilizers created a wrongful birth cause of action against the pharmacist, with damages recoverable for pregnancy, birth, and childrearing costs), <u>lv. denied</u>, 385 Mich. 753 (1971). While judicial exceptions to standard tort law doctrines should "express the manifest will of the people," <u>Troppi</u>, 31 Mich. App. at 252, 187 N.W.2d at 516, the trial court's declaration that a child's birth is always a "blessing" reflects only the crusading paternalism of a bygone era.

The Bell-Wesleys' determination that Scott would undergo a vasectomy was an intimate, personal family planning matter that

6

falls within the zone of privacy and self-determination
protected by the Constitution. <u>See Griswold v. Connecticut</u>,
381 U.S. 479 (1965); <u>Roe v. Wade</u>, 410 U.S. 113 (1973). Rebecca
and Scott had a fundamental right to determine not to have
children. <u>Rivera v. State</u>, 94 Misc. 2d 157, 162, 404 N.Y.S.2d
950, 953 (1978) (negligent tubal ligation operation created
malpractice cause of action for damages for medical expenses,
pain and suffering, and costs of raising an unwanted child).
O'Toole's repeated negligence thwarted their exercise of this
right. When a doctor's negligence "results in the birth of an
unwanted child, a substantial interference with the fundamental
rights of the parents occurs," and the courts should recognize
its significance. <u>Id.</u>, 94 Misc. 2d at 162, 404 N.Y.S.2d at
953. Public policy prohibits allowing an exception to tort
liability where "the impact of such an exception would impair
the exercise of a constitutionallly protected right." <u>Ochs v.
Borrelli</u>, 187 Conn. 253, 256, 445 A.2d 883, 885 (1982)
(negligent tubal ligation).[1]

---

[1] Refusal by Ames' courts to recognize the Bell-Wesleys'
wrongful birth claim could itself be seen as a violation of the
couple's right to self-determination. At least one court has
held that "since the State may not infringe upon this right, it
may not constitutionally denigrate the right by completely
denying protection provided as a matter of course to like
rights." <u>Troppi</u>, 31 Mich. App. at 253-254, 187 N.W.2d at 517;
<u>Rivera</u>, 94 Misc. 2d at 162, 404 N.Y.S.2d at 954. <u>Cf. Shelley
v. Kraemer</u>, 334 U.S. 1 (1948) (court enforcement of racially
restrictive covenant is state action).

Negligent physicians like Dr. O'Toole must not be allowed to escape the consequences of their carelessness. Recognition of a wrongful birth cause of action is necessary to deter negligence and to insure a proper standard of medical care. Faced with a blameworthy defendant, O'Toole, and his innocent victims, the Bell-Wesleys, it is in society's best interest to compensate the victims for their losses, rather than to grant the tortfeasor immunity. Fairness requires that Dr. O'Toole pay for the consequences of his wrongful behavior, rather than force his innocent victims to absorb the costs of his negligence. See generally Note, Wrongful Conception: Who Pays for Bringing Up Baby?, 47 Fordham L. Rev. 418 (1978-79).

Recognition of the Bell-Wesleys' wrongful birth claim would in no way denigrate the value of Frank Bell's life. Frank is not an item of damage in this suit. The issue is not Frank or the love his parents feel for him, but the negligence that led to his birth, denied the Bell-Wesleys the opportunity to lead their chosen lifestyle, and imposed upon them burdens that they were entitled to avoid through sterilization.

Recognition of the Bell-Wesleys' claim will not result in psychological harm to a child who discovers that he was unplanned. Frank could easily be protected from this unlikely event by keeping the names involved in this action confidential. Most importantly, recovery by the Bell-Wesleys will inure to Frank's emotional benefit, since it will relieve "the economic pressure of raising an unexpected child and

8

permit the parents to concentrate on giving the child the love and care he or she needs." Boone v. Mullendore, 416 So. 2d 718, 724-25 (Ala. 1982) (recognizing wrongful birth claim for birth of healthy but unplanned child) (Faulkner, J., concurring).

Rebecca and Scott Bell-Wesley have demonstrated all of the elements that constitute medical malpractice, and are entitled to recover for the extensive injuries caused by defendant's negligence. Any exception from standard tort law that immunized O'Toole would victimize Frank Bell's innocent parents and contravene public policies favoring family planning and self-determination, discouraging careless behavior, and redressing harms.

II. DR. O'TOOLE MUST BE HELD LIABLE TO THE BELL-WESLEYS FOR ALL OF THE DAMAGES FLOWING FROM HIS REPEATED NEGLIGENCE.

A. The Bell-Wesleys Should Be Compensated For All Their Injuries, Including Sterilization Costs, Pre-natal and Post-natal Medical Expenses, Emotional and Physical Pain and Suffering, Financial Sacrifices, and the Costs of Raising Their Unplanned Child.

Rebecca and Scott Bell-Wesley are entitled to recover for all of the injuries resulting from Dr. O'Toole's defective sterilization operation and sperm count, including their pain and suffering, emotional trauma, lost earnings, the costs of raising Frank, and the sacrifice of their chosen lifestyle. The standard formula for tort remedies should apply to this wrongful birth claim as it does to any medical malpractice action; Dr. O'Toole must be held liable for all injuries flowing naturally and foreseeably from his repeated negligence. See W. Prosser, supra p. 4, at § 43. The obvious consequences of a negligently performed sterilization are the conception and birth of an unplanned child and the associated costs of pregnancy, birth, and upbringing. See Custodio v. Bauer, 251 Cal. App. 2d 303, 322-23, 59 Cal. Rptr. 463, 476-77 (1967) (valid wrongful birth claim arising from negligent tubal ligation).

The Bell-Wesleys should recover for each of the injuries which O'Toole has inflicted upon them because the fundamental aim of tort recovery is to place the victim in the same position she would have been in had the tort never occurred. The Superior Court's failure to acknowledge the Bell-Wesleys' cause of action has left uncompensated significant emotional and economic harms. The medical expenses associated with Rebecca's pregnancy and Frank's birth are costs that the Bell-Wesleys would not have incurred but for O'Toole's malfeasance. Pre- and post-natal medical expenses are generally awarded in wrongful birth actions. See, e.g., Sherlock, 260 N.W.2d at 175; Custodio, 251 Cal. App. 2d at 322-23, 59 Cal. Rptr. at 476-77. Moreover, Rebecca endured great physical pain and both Scott and Rebecca suffered loss of consortium in connection with the pregnancy, injuries for which they are entitled to further damages. See Sherlock, 260 N.W.2d at 175.

The Bell-Wesleys suffered acute mental anguish after learning that Rebecca was pregnant. Scott and Rebecca had experienced three other pregnancies, each resulting in deformed children who died shortly after birth. O'Toole himself had informed them that any future pregnancy was seventy-five percent likely to have similarly tragic results. Thus, for over eight months, the Bell-Wesleys lived in fear that Rebecca would give birth to another deformed child. Their damage award should reflect the mental suffering O'Toole's negligence inflicted. See Ochs, 187 Conn. at 257, 445 A.2d at 886 (recognizing that fear of the birth of a handicapped child is a compensable injury); Hartke, 707 F.2d at 1555 (mother's anxiety about unborn child's potential deformity merited damage award).

Both Scott and Rebecca have lost and will continue to lose valuable time and earnings in their chosen careers. Rebecca's leave of absence from her position as Assistant Attorney General has deprived her of valuable career experiences necessary to her professional development and may have jeopardized her job. (R.7) As the Superior Court noted, the defendant's negligence has profoundly altered the Bell-Wesleys' lifestyle. (R.8) Frank's birth and the resulting responsibilities have greatly curtailed the financial and emotional freedom the couple enjoyed. The Bell-Wesleys should be compensated for this economic and emotional strain. See Custodio, 251 Cal. App. 2d at 322-24, 59 Cal. Rptr. at 476-77.

11

O'Toole's tortious conduct has thrust the extensive financial burden of raising a child upon Scott and Rebecca. They seek to recover not for Frank's life, but for the diminution in family wealth which necessarily resulted from his birth. See id., 251 Cal. App. 2d at 324, 59 Cal. Rptr. at 477. The costs of raising Frank "are a direct financial injury to the parents, no different in immediate effect than the medical expenses resulting from the wrongful conception and birth of the child." Sherlock, 260 N.W.2d at 175. Government studies of the economic costs of raising children provide a reasonable basis for judicial assessment of the extent of this injury. (R.4) Therefore, Rebecca and Scott should recover for the costs of rearing Frank.

Recovery for all emotional and pecuniary costs is necessary to compensate the Bell-Wesleys for the full extent of their injuries and to hold O'Toole liable for the complete consequences of his negligence. This recovery is not disproportionate to the actions of Dr. O'Toole; the doctor could easily have limited his liability by taking the simple step of providing proper post-operative care. Full recovery by wrongful birth claimants is necessary to sufficiently deter negligence in performing vasectomies. Courts must assess doctors for the full costs of their malfeasance in order to provide adequate incentives for safe, effective medical procedures. See Kingsbury v. Smith, 122 N.H. 237, 242, 442 A.2d 1003, 1005 (1982) (failure to recognize wrongful birth

claims would "[dilute] the standard of professional conduct and
expertise in the area of family planning").

    B.   The "Benefits Rule" Does Not Warrant Offset of the
          Bell-Wesleys' Damages Because Any Benefits Received
          Affect a Different Interest Than That Harmed By
          O'Tool's Negligence.

The extensive damages to the Bell-Wesleys should not be
offset by any benefits they received through the birth of their
unplanned child. Courts have sometimes permitted such an
offset, purporting to rely upon the "benefits rule" of section
920 of the Restatement (Second) of Torts. See, e.g., Stills v.
Gratton, 55 Cal. App. 3d 698, 707-09, 127 Cal. Rptr. 652,
658-59 (1976). Section 920 provides:

> When the defendant's tortious conduct has
> caused harm to the plaintiff or to his property
> and in doing so has conferred a special benefit
> to the interest of the plaintiff that was
> harmed, the value of the benefit conferred is
> considered in mitigation of damages, to the
> extent that this is equitable.

Restatement (Second) of Torts, § 920 (1972) (emphasis added). The
birth of an unplanned, unwanted child undoubtedly confers some
benefits upon the Bell-Wesleys. Nonetheless, these benefits cannot
mitigate the Bell-Wesleys' injuries because they involve interests
distinct from those harmed by O'Toole's misconduct. The equitable
considerations embodied in the benefits rule bar offsetting these
benefits against the Bell-Wesleys' damage award.

    The emotional benefits the Bell-Wesleys received through the
"joys of parenthood" are of an entirely different nature and kind

13

than the financial injuries and the pain and suffering inflicted on them by O'Toole's negligence. Rebecca and Scott's deep love for Frank does not negate the fact that his birth was neither planned nor desired. Their affection for Frank will not provide the Bell-Wesleys with the money to cover his expenses or replace the time and energy diverted from their careers. When "[p]roperly applied in the wrongful birth context, the benefit rule would allow the recovery for emotional harm to be offset only by an emotional benefit, the recovery for an economic harm to be offset only by an economic benefit, and so on." Comment, Judicial Limitations on Damages Recoverable for the Wrongful Birth of a Healthy Infant, 68 Va. L. Rev. 1311, 1326 (1982). The examples provided in the Restatement indicate that the drafters supported distinguishing between emotional, physical, and pecuniary interests when applying the benefits rule. Restatement (Second) of Torts, § 920, comment b, illustrations 4 and 6 (1972). The Bell-Wesleys' love for Frank will not heal the injuries to their economic and professional situation. At most, the "joys" of parenthood could offset only the emotional burden directly associated with raising Frank. In no event should any benefits be offset against the injuries Scott and Rebecca experienced up to and including the time of Frank's birth, since they could receive no benefit from the child before he was born. See Sherlock, 260 N.W.2d at 175-76 (allowing offset of benefits only against rearing costs); Kingsbury, 122 N.H. at 243, 442 A.2d at 1005 (1982) (denying offset against sterilization and pregnancy costs); see also Hartke, 707 F.2d at 1557 n.16.

14

Offsetting the benefits of parenthood against the Bell-Wesleys' injuries would pervert the equitable result contemplated by section 920. Rebecca and Scott elected to exercise their fundamental right of self-determination to <u>avoid</u> the joys of parenthood. The Bell-Wesleys' loss of control over their lifestyle which resulted from O'Toole's careless misconduct cannot be compensated by any benefits associated with raising Frank. Section 920's purpose is to keep the victim from recovering more than the harm incurred, ". . . and not to permit the tortfeasor to force a benefit on him against his will." Restatement (Second) of Torts, § 920, comment f (1972). <u>See also</u> Kashi, <u>The Case of the Unwanted Blessing: Wrongful Life</u>, 31 U. Miami L. Rev. 1409, 1415 (1977) (characterizing doctor-conferred benefits in wrongful birth cases as "officious intermeddling"). O'Toole cannot be permitted to escape liability for the serious injuries he has inflicted upon the Bell-Wesleys because he has forced upon them a "benefit" which they obtained a vasectomy specifically to avoid.

    C.   <u>The Bell-Wesleys Were Not Obligated to Abort Their Child, to Place Him for Adoption, or to Submit to Amniocentesis Because They Were Required Only to Take Reasonable Steps to Mitigate Their Damages.</u>

O'Toole could not require the Bell-Wesleys to undergo amniocentesis, to abort Frank, or to place him up for adoption. The couple was obligated only to take reasonable steps to mitigate the damages caused by O'Toole's negligence. <u>See</u> Restatement (Second) of Torts, § 918; McCormick, <u>Handbook on the Law of Damages</u> § 35

(1935). Abortion, adoption, and amniocentesis go far beyond reasonable mitigation of damages.

O'Toole has no right to insist that Rebecca "have the emotional and mental makeup of a woman who is willing to abort" her child. Troppi, 31 Mich. App. at 260, 187 N.W.2d at 520. Rebecca and Scott declined to abort their child on moral grounds. (R.8) A rule of law which ignored their beliefs and required Rebecca to have an abortion "would constitute an invasion of privacy of the grossest and most pernicious kind." Rivera, 94 Misc. 2d at 163, 404 N.Y.S.2d at 954. "The right to have an abortion may not automatically be converted to an obligation to have one" in order to mitigate wrongful birth damages. Ziemba v. Sternberg, 45 A.D.2d 230, 233, 357 N.Y.S.2d 265, 269 (1974).

Requiring Scott and Rebecca to place Frank up for adoption would ignore the natural bonds of parenthood established during the nine month term of pregnancy. See Clapham v. Yanga, 102 Mich. App. 47, 61, 300 N.W.2d 727, 733 (1981) (familial ties held to render mitigation by adoption unreasonable even where claimants were grandparents who voluntarily took and cared for the child). While the Bell-Wesleys had made a conscious choice not to conceive a child, their natural affection for Frank renders placement for adoption unreasonable. To force the Bell-Wesleys to part with another child after the loss of their first three children would compound the emotional trauma caused by defendant's carelessness.

The Bell-Wesleys' decision to forego amniocentesis was reasonable in light of the surrounding circumstances. Amniocentesis

16

involves analysis of amniotic fluid obtained by the insertion of an eight-inch needle into the mother's abdomen. We now know that submission to this painful process would have revealed that the unplanned child was normal. When Scott and Rebecca made their decision, however, they knew only that it was highly probable that the child was deformed. (R.1) They were unwilling to abort the child in any circumstance. Therefore, submission to the test was likely only to increase the couple's suffering by confirming that Rebecca would give birth to a deformed child. The Bell-Wesleys behaved reasonably in avoiding this additional trauma.

CONCLUSION

Dr. O'Toole's repeated negligence caused the Bell-Wesleys substantial physical, financial, and emotional injuries that were left uncompensated by the Superior Court. Therefore, this court should reverse the judgment of the Superior Court and award full recovery to Rebecca and Scott Bell-Wesley.

Respectfully submitted,

Jane E. Harvey

Jane E. Harvey
Attorney for Plaintiff-Appellants

IN THE SUPREME COURT OF THE
STATE OF AMES

Civil Action No. 90-2004

SCOTT AND REBECCA BELL-WESLEY, Plaintiff-Appellants

v.

DR. STEPHEN O'TOOLE, Defendant-Appellee

BRIEF FOR THE DEFENDANT-APPELLEE

D. Nathan Neuville
Attorney for the Appellee

Argument: March 22, 1991
Ames Courtroom
7:30 p.m.

TABLE OF CONTENTS

TABLE OF CITATIONS

CASES

MISCELLANEOUS

QUESTIONS PRESENTED

Should a "wrongful birth" cause of action be created for the birth of a normal child to parents who had long wanted a child and who sought sterilization solely to avoid bearing a deformed child?

If a "wrongful birth" claim is created, should the damages claimed by the parents be offset by the extensive benefits they derive from their healthy child or reduced due to the parents' failure to mitigate damages through the reasonable measures of amniocentesis and adoption?

STATEMENT OF FACTS

Appellants Rebecca and Scott Bell-Wesley brought suit in the Superior Court of the State of Ames against Dr. Stephen O'Toole, an established Ames physician, seeking damages for the birth of a healthy, normal child following an unsuccessful sterilization.

Mr. and Ms. Bell-Wesley are a successful professional couple residing in Holmes, Ames. Scott Bell-Wesley is an architect, and Rebecca Bell-Wesley is an Assistant Attorney General for the State of Ames. On three occasions before the January 1990 birth of their son, Frank Michael Bell, the

Bell-Wesleys had attempted to start a family. Each time, however, Ms. Bell-Wesley gave birth to a congenitally deformed infant that died within six months of birth. (R.1) Dr. O'Toole informed the Bell-Wesleys that there was a seventy-five percent chance that any child they conceived would suffer the same deformity. For the sole purpose of avoiding the conception of another deformed child, the Bell-Wesleys decided to have Dr. O'Toole sterilize Mr. Bell-Wesley. (R.8)

On October 16, 1988, Dr. O'Toole performed a vasectomy on Mr. Bell-Wesley. (R.8) After a follow-up sperm count, Dr. O'Toole mistakenly informed Mr. Bell-Wesley that he was sterile. (R.10) Six months after the vasectomy, Ms. Bell-Wesley discovered that she was pregnant. Ms. Bell-Wesley refused to undergo amniocentesis, a simple procedure that would have revealed that the fetus she carried was normal in every respect. (R.6,9) On January 4, 1990, Ms. Bell-Wesley gave birth to healthy, normal son, Frank Michael Bell. (R.8) While they characterize Frank as an "unwanted" child, the Bell-Wesleys have declined to put him up for adoption. (R.9)

Although they profess great love for their son, the Bell-Wesleys brought suit against Dr. O'Toole, claiming to be injured by Frank's birth. The Bell-Wesleys seek damages of approximately $566,000 to cover items such as injury to their "lifestyle" and the financial and emotional costs of raising Frank. (R.2-3) Judge Nancy Llewenstein of the Superior Court found that the vasectomy was unsuccessful and that the sperm

count was negligently performed. (R.10) The court awarded the
Bell-Wesleys damages for the out-of-pocket costs, pain and
suffering, and loss of consortium incident to the vasectomy.
Id. The court refused to allow a wrongful birth cause of
action for the costs incident to Rebecca's pregnancy and the
birth and rearing of Frank Bell, holding that the benefits to
the Bell-Wesleys of this healthy, normal child outweigh any
attendant costs. (R.11) The Bell-Wesleys appeal the Superior
Court decision.

ARGUMENT

I. THE COURT SHOULD NOT CREATE A WRONGFUL BIRTH CAUSE OF ACTION
    FOR THE BELL-WESLEYS BECAUSE THE BIRTH OF THEIR HEALTHY,
    NORMAL SON AFTER THEY SOUGHT STERILIZATION SOLELY TO AVOID A
    DEFORMED CHILD WAS A BLESSING, NOT AN INJURY.

The Bell-Wesleys cannot recover for "wrongful birth" because
Frank Bell's birth was a blessing, not an injury. The Bell-
Wesleys have failed to demonstrate an indispensable element of
their tort claim: a legally recognizable injury. W. Prosser,
Law of Torts § 30 (4th ed. 1971). While the Bell-Wesleys
characterize their son's birth as a harm, many jurisdictions
have denied that a healthy child's birth can ever be an injury
to its parents. The birth of a normal son to parents who
procured a vasectomy solely to avoid having a deformed child is
not an injury, even under the rationales adopted by courts
recognizing wrongful birth claims. Furthermore, a number of

serious public policy concerns preclude labeling Frank's birth an injury.

The Bell-Wesleys have suffered no injury. For years they yearned for a healthy child like Frank. Before Frank's birth, the Bell-Wesleys had tried to start a family on three separate occasions, only to see each attempt result in the birth of a deformed, short-lived child. (R.1) The Bell-Wesleys abandoned their hopes of having a family only when Dr. O'Toole informed them that it was highly probable that any child they conceived would suffer the same deformity. Scott Bell-Wesley obtained a vasectomy solely to avoid the birth of another deformed child. (R.8) The birth of a healthy child, especially in light of the deaths of their earlier children, is a great benefit to the Bell-Wesleys. The Bell-Wesleys proclaim that they love their child deeply, yet they now style Frank's birth an "injury." It is difficult to believe that they would make this characterization absent the prospect of pecuniary gain. As Judge Llewenstein concluded, under these circumstances Frank's birth can only be seen as a blessing. (R.11)

The notion that the Bell-Wesleys were injured by the birth of a healthy child "offends . . . fundamental values attached to human life." Cockrum v. Baumgartner, 95 Ill. 2d 193, 198, 447 N.E.2d 385, 388 (1983) (refusing to recognize a cause of action for the birth of a healthy child after a negligent vasectomy). Many courts, reasoning that "the value of a human life outweighs any 'damage' which might be said to follow from the fact of

4

birth," have held that a healthy child's birth is never an injury, regardless of the circumstances. Coleman v. Garrison, 349 A.2d 8, 13 (Del. 1975); see also Public Health Trust v. Brown, 388 So. 2d 1084 (Fla. App. 1980). Because the Bell-Wesleys actually desired a healthy child, this Court need not go so far as to proclaim that a child's birth can never be an injury in order to conclude that the value of life forbids labeling Frank's birth an injury.

The circumstances of Frank's birth stand in sharp contrast to the situations in which wrongful birth claims have been recognized because the Bell-Wesleys have escaped the injury they sought to avoid. Courts have sometimes recognized wrongful birth claims where the parents, like the Bell-Wesleys, sought sterilization for eugenic or therapeutic reasons. However, they have done so only where the child's birth has resulted in the deformity or other physical injury the parents intended to guard against. Compare, e.g., Ochs v. Borrelli, 187 Conn. 253, 445 A.2d 883 (1982) (recognizing claim for birth of child with mild orthopedic defects after negligent sterilization operation), with Christensen v. Thornby, 192 Minn. 123, 255 N.W. 620 (1934) (where the purpose of sterilization was to prevent physical risk to the mother, the birth, without complications, of a healthy infant was not actionable). The Bell-Wesleys sought only to avoid the birth of a fourth deformed child; they cannot recover for the birth of the healthy, normal child they always wanted.

The Bell-Wesleys did not obtain a vasectomy because they felt they could not afford a child or because they wished to limit the size of their family, two other situations in which courts have recognized wrongful birth claims. Some courts have permitted recovery for wrongful birth where a child is born after a non-therapeutic sterilization because the child represents the very thing its parents sought to avoid: an economic drain on family resources or a simple increase in family size. See, e.g., Sherlock v. Stillwater Clinic, 260 N.W.2d 169 (Minn. 1977) (sterilization sought in order to limit family size after birth of seventh child); Betancourt v. Gaylor, 136 N.J. Super. 69, 74, 344 A.2d 336, 339 (1975) (parents sought to avoid expense of additional child). Scott and Rebecca Bell-Wesley, however, decided upon sterilization for purely therapeutic reasons. These two professionals sought for years to expand their family and are well able to provide for their son. No court has ever permitted recovery for wrongful birth under such circumstances.

The Bell-Wesleys' constitutional privacy rights under Griswold v. Connecticut, 381 U.S. 479 (1965), and Roe v. Wade, 410 U.S. 113 (1973), are not at issue in this lawsuit. Contra Appellants' Brief at 6-7. Roe and Griswold establish privacy rights which protect the Bell-Wesleys only against "state action" or government intrusion. See, e.g., Roe, 410 U.S. at 153. There has been no state action against the Bell-Wesleys; Dr. O'Toole is a private individual, not a government agent.

The Bell-Wesleys' privacy rights are also uninfringed because the couple procured a vasectomy for therapeutic reasons, not for the purpose of limiting family size. Roe and Griswold articulate the right of parents to control their family's size. The Bell-Wesleys, however, have consistently sought to increase their family's size, not to limit it.

Recognizing the Bell-Wesleys' cause of action would undermine important notions of parental responsibility and risk causing Frank severe emotional trauma. The prospect of financial gain will induce parents to proclaim publicly that their child's birth was an injury. Encouraging such claims will adversely affect family structure. To recover for wrongful birth, parents would have to "demonstrate not only that they did not want the child," but also that "the child remains an uncherished, unwanted burden." Cockrum, 95 Ill. 2d at 202, 447 N.E.2d at 390. Parents will resent and be alienated from children that they have been encouraged to view as injuries; they will accept their obligations towards such children grudgingly. When a child such as Frank learns that he was unwanted, that his parents felt injured by his birth, and that they were unwilling to pay for his expenses themselves, he will suffer serious emotional injury. Our society has not become so "sophisticated" as to "dismiss [the] emotional trauma [of a child] as nonsense." Wilbur v. Kerr, 275 Ark. 239, 244, 628 S.W.2d 568, 571 (1982) (denying recovery for the expense of raising an unwanted, healthy child).

7

The recovery the Bell-Wesleys seek is not commensurate with Dr. O'Toole's culpability. See Rieck v. Medical Protective Co., 64 Wis. 2d 514, 518-19, 219 N.W.2d 242, 244-45 (1974) (excessive burden on physician and other public policy concerns preclude recovery for birth of unwanted child). The costs of raising Frank to adulthood, estimated by the Bell-Wesleys at over $235,000, (R.4), are astronomical in comparison to those involved in a vasectomy, a low-cost operation performed in the doctor's own office. The goal of deterrence has already been adequately served by the Superior Court's award of damages and, more importantly, by the accompanying injury to Dr. O'Toole's professional reputation. To go beyond the trial court's award and assess liability which is grossly disproportionate to Dr. O'Toole's negligence will result in the practice of "defensive" medicine and in increased sterilization costs. Faced by the prospect of devastatingly disproportionate liability and dramatically increased insurance costs, physicians may counsel against sterilization when the operation is in their patient's best interest. Physicians will pass their increased costs on to their patients by charging greater fees for sterilization, denying a socially valuable family planning option to low-income patients.[1]

---

[1] Ironically, some courts have justified liability for wrongful birth by noting that public policy favors contraception. See, e.g., Sherlock, 260 N.W.2d at 175; see also Appellants' Brief at 5. As this analysis demonstrates, imposition of liability will have a detrimental effect upon the

Because the Bell-Wesleys did not procure sterilization for financial reasons, allowing them to recover the costs of raising Frank would grant them a "windfall." See Hartke v. McKelway, 707 F.2d 1544, 1553-55 (D.C. Cir. 1983), cert. denied, 104 S.Ct. 425 (1983); Rieck, 64 Wis. 2d at 518-19, 219 N.W.2d at 244-45. The Bell-Wesleys will enjoy every benefit, tangible and intangible, associated with raising a healthy child whom they adore. Meanwhile, Dr. O'Toole and, via insurance, the rest of society, will be forced to bear all of the costs intertwined with these benefits. The Bell-Wesleys never sought to avoid these costs and are fully capable of bearing them. Recognition of their wrongful birth claim would unjustly enrich the Bell-Wesleys.

Creating a wrongful birth cause of action for the Bell-Wesleys would threaten the emotional well-being of children, have deleterious effects upon family structure, and impose excessive liability upon physicians. It might be possible to ignore these concerns where the wrongful birth claimants could not provide for their child's needs or where the child was unhealthy. The Bell-Wesleys, however, are financially capable and have become the parents of the healthy child they desired. To find that the birth of this normal child injured a couple that sought sterilization only to avoid a deformed child would be a radical deviation from the common law, including that

─────────────────────

goal of universally attainable contraception.

of states recognizing wrongful birth claims. The Bell-Wesleys'
attempt to fashion a wrongful birth cause of action out of
these circumstances must be rejected.

II. THE BENEFITS RESULTING FROM FRANK BELL'S BIRTH AND HIS
     PARENTS' FAILURE TO MITIGATE DAMAGES PRECLUDE THE
     BELL-WESLEYS FROM RECOVERING DAMAGES EXCEEDING THOSE
     AWARDED BY THE SUPERIOR COURT.

     A.   The Benefits the Bell-Wesleys Derive From the Birth of
          Their Son Outweigh All Costs Associated With His Birth
          and Rearing, Barring Recovery For Those Costs Under the
          Benefits Rule.

     Even if the Bell-Wesleys' claim is recognized, they are entitled
to no further damages because the benefits accruing to them from
Frank's birth outweigh any purported injuries. The benefits rule of
the Restatement (Second) of Torts provides:

> Where the defendant's tortious conduct has
> caused harm to the plaintiff or to his property
> and in so doing has conferred upon the
> plaintiff a special benefit to the interest
> which was harmed, the value of the benefit
> conferred is considered in mitigation of
> damages, where this is equitable.

Restatement (Second) of Torts, § 920 (1972). Every
jurisdiction recognizing wrongful birth claims employs the
benefits rule to offset the benefits of parenthood against any
injuries. See, e.g., University of Arizona Health Sciences
Center v. Superior Court of Maricopa County, 136 Ariz. 579,
584-86, 667 P.2d 1294, 1299-1301 (1983); Troppi v. Scarf, 31
Mich. App. 240, 254-57, 187 N.W.2d 511, 517-18 (1971), lv.
denied, 385 Mich. 753 (1971). Numerous courts have held that

10

the benefits of a healthy, normal child outweigh the costs of rearing her as a matter of law. The Bell-Wesleys' own evaluation of the costs and benefits of parenthood, evident from their repeated attempts to have a healthy child, demonstrates that Frank's birth was, on balance, a benefit to them. Any further damage award would unjustly enrich the Bell-Wesleys at Dr. O'Toole's expense.

Frank's birth will bring his parents all the joy and satisfaction normally associated with parenthood. The equitable principle embodied in the benefits rule requires that the Bell-Wesleys' damages be offset by the "value of the child's aid, comfort, and society which will benefit the parents for the duration of their lives." Sherlock, 260 N.W.2d at 176. While these benefits are great, they are also largely intangible and elude financial calculation. To place a dollar value upon these benefits would be to denigrate the value of the child's life. Many courts have recognized that these benefits cannot and should not be subject to judicial assessment; they have concluded that the incalculable benefits received by the parents outweigh the costs of raising a healthy child as a matter of law. See Beardsley v. Wierdsma, 650 P.2d 288, 293 (Wyo. 1982) (any attempt to measure these benefits would be a "misplaced attempt to put a specific dollar value on a child's life"); see also Cockrum, 95 Ill. 2d at 200-01, 447 N.E.2d at 388-89; Terrell v. Garcia, 496 S.W.2d 124, 128 (Tex. Civ. App. 1973), cert. denied, 415 U.S. 927 (1974).

11

Even if the benefits of a healthy child were not held to outweigh the costs in every case, the Bell-Wesleys' demonstrated desire for a healthy child requires a holding that the benefits predominate in this case. Correct application of the benefits rule requires examination of all the circumstances surrounding the parents' wrongful birth claim. Troppi, 31 Mich. App. at 254-57, 187 N.W.2d at 518-19. When the Bell-Wesleys conceived each of their three deceased children they had determined that the joys of parenthood exceeded the emotional and financial costs of pregnancy, birth, and child-rearing. Nothing indicates that the Bell-Wesleys ever altered their evaluation; they sought sterilization solely because they feared the birth of a fourth deformed child. (R.8) The purpose for which the parents sought sterilization is the most telling evidence of whether, on balance, the child's birth actually damaged the couple. See University of Arizona, 136 Ariz. at 585, 667 P.2d at 1300; Hartke, 707 F.2d 1544. Because the Bell-Wesleys' purpose was to avoid a deformed child, the birth of their normal son has not damaged them.

The Bell-Wesleys' subsequent behavior indicates that they do not feel injured by Frank's existence. They stress their love for Frank, Appellants' Brief at 3, 14, and decline to place him for adoption. See Public Health Trust, 388 So. 2d at 1086 (failure to place the child for adoption indicates that the parents are benefited by keeping the child). Moreover,

12

they have not altered their lifestyle greatly since Scott
Bell-Wesley's vasectomy. The only visible change in the
Bell-Wesleys' circumstances is Rebecca's new position. Ms.
Bell-Wesley had held this job for less than six months when she
discovered she was pregnant. Her affection for Frank
demonstrates that she did not become so caught up in her new
position during this short period that she abandoned her desire
for a child. This couple desperately wished to have a healthy
child of their own; Frank's arrival was a long-hoped-for
blessing.

The Bell-Wesleys' desire for a child is hardly surprising,
since child-rearing will place a relatively slight burden upon
them. As an architect and a lawyer, Mr. and Ms. Bell-Wesley
will have no difficulty supporting Frank financially. The
Bell-Wesleys have no other children, so Frank's birth will not
deprive any siblings of parental care or support. For years
the couple has been fully prepared to accept the economic and
emotional costs of raising a child, yet the list of damages
that they now claim is no more than a catalogue of the costs
normally associated with bearing and raising a child. The
Bell-Wesleys' own assessment of parenthood establishes that the
benefits of Frank's birth outweigh these costs.

Recognition of the enormous benefits associated with
Frank's birth is not precluded by the benefits rule's
requirement that the benefits be "to the interest of the
plaintiff which was harmed." Restatement (Second) of Torts,

13

§ 920 (1972). Courts applying this equitable principle in wrongful birth cases generally offset all of the costs involved by all of the benefits. See, e.g., Troppi, 31 Mich. App. at 255, 187 N.W.2d at 518; see also Comment, Judicial Limitations on Damages Recoverable for the Wrongful Birth of a Healthy Infant, 68 Va. L. Rev. 1311 (1982). While it may be conceptually possible to distinguish between the Bell-Wesleys' economic and emotional interests in Frank's birth, the practical reality is that these interests are inextricably intertwined. See University of Arizona, 136 Ariz. at 584 & n.4, 667 P.2d at 1299 & n.4; Troppi, 31 Mich. App. at 255, 187 N.W.2d at 518. There is no jurisdiction in which these interests are separated in applying the benefits rule to a wrongful birth claim.[2] The equitable rule against unjust enrichment, embodied in the benefits rule, compels the offset of all the benefits of Frank's birth against all of the costs.

Furthermore, Frank's presence benefits the interests the Bell-Wesleys claim were harmed. While they allege injury to their "childless lifestyle," their persistent attempts at childbearing demonstrate that Frank enhances their lifestyle. Frank will even provide future financial benefits; "a child is

---

[2] The only case in which economic and emotional interests were distinguished when applying the benefits rule in a wrongful birth context was subsequently reversed. See Cockrum v. Baumgartner, 99 Ill. App. 3d 271, 425 N.W.2d 968 (1982), rev'd 95 Ill. 2d 193, 447 N.E.2d 385 (1983).

some security for the parents' old age." <u>Terrell</u>, 496 S.W.2d at
128. Failure to offset the benefits of Frank's birth based on
a "same interest" rationale will unjustly enrich the
Bell-Wesleys, producing a result antithetical to the benefits
rule.

    B.   <u>The Bell-Wesleys' Failure to Mitigate Their Damages
Through the Reasonable Steps of Amniocentesis and
Adoption Precludes Further Recovery</u>.

The Bell-Wesleys are also barred from any further recovery
because of their failure to mitigate their damages. They may
not recover damages for injuries resulting from an
unintentional tort when they could have avoided that harm
through reasonable effort. Restatement (Second) of Torts,
§ 918 (1972). Amniocentesis and adoption were reasonable steps
that would have eliminated virtually all of the damages the
Bell-Wesleys seek to recover. The Bell-Wesleys cannot force
Dr. O'Toole to compensate them for injuries they could have
avoided by fulfilling their duty to mitigate damages.

Amniocentesis would have eliminated any emotional trauma
Mr. and Ms. Bell-Wesley experienced due to fear that their
child would be deformed. The trial court determined that this
safe, simple procedure would have revealed that Frank was
healthy and free of deformity. (R.9) Under the circumstances,
having amniocentesis performed was the most reasonable measure
for the Bell-Wesleys to take. Even had Frank been deformed,
knowledge of this would have caused the Bell-Wesleys no more

15

emotional trauma than that caused by the uncertainty suffered before Frank's birth. On the other hand, the discovery that Frank was normal would have prevented any emotional suffering. Given the ease with which the Bell-Wesleys could have avoided emotional trauma, that element must be eliminated from any evaluation of the Bell-Wesleys' damages.

If the Bell-Wesleys were actually burdened more than they were benefited by Frank's birth, the reasonable step to mitigate their damages was to put the child up for adoption. To justify an award of damages to the Bell-Wesleys, it would be necessary to find that the personal ties between parent and child which society normally presumes to be of great value, were insufficiently valuable to the Bell-Wesleys to offset the costs of bearing and raising a child. See discussion supra, p. 10. If the Bell-Wesleys place so little value upon the parent-child relationship that a normal, healthy child represents a net burden to them, it was unreasonable for them to refuse to put the child up for adoption. Frank would be better off in a home with adoptive parents who cherish their relationship with him and who regard themselves as better off with than without him. By their own estimation, the Bell-Wesleys would be better off as well. If it is unreasonable to ask the Bell-Wesleys to give Frank Bell up for adoption, it is because they do, in fact, derive a greater benefit than burden from parenthood.

The Bell-Wesleys' failure to mitigate their damages by undergoing amniocentesis or placing Frank for adoption precludes them from recovering the damage which could have been avoided by these steps.

CONCLUSION

For the foregoing reasons, the judgment of the Superior Court should be affirmed.

Respectfully submitted,

D. Nathan Neuville
Attorney for the Appellee

Chapter V

ORAL ADVOCACY

After the research is done and the brief is written comes the culmination of your efforts—the oral argument. Going into court and trying to persuade judges to find in your client's behalf is a different challenge from writing the brief, and learning to deliver an effective argument takes practice. Preparation is crucial to a successful argument. If you know your case and your arguments, you will be ready to confidently answer the questions presented to you, even those you never expected.

Oral argument is an important part of the American tradition of advocacy. In the early years of the Supreme Court, arguments lasted for hours, if not days. While caseload pressures have reduced the amount of time available to today's advocates for oral argument, it nonetheless presents a valuable opportunity to convince the court of the merits of the case and to dispel any lingering doubts a particular judge may have.

The basic structure of an appellate oral argument is simple and direct. The appellant rises first to give a short introduction to the nature and facts of the case, and then to explain why the court should reverse the lower tribunal's decision. The appellee then presents his side of the case. Finally, the appellant has an opportunity to rebut her opponent's assertions. Throughout the argument the judges are likely to interrupt counsels' presentations with questions. By listening carefully to the judges' questions, the advocates can discover how a judge perceives the case and immediately respond to those perceptions. The process is dynamic and complex, and many have said that it is an art truly mastered by only a few appellate lawyers.

As in briefwriting, styles and approaches to oral advocacy are quite diverse, and again there is no "right" way to prepare for and present your case. However, the crux of your presentation must be a solid and well-prepared argument. Especially in a first-year moot court program, judges are not so much interested in the flamboyant or dramatic nature with which you present your argument as they are in the actual substance of your presentation and your prowess in answering their questions. Of course some drama can be helpful. But be sure to know your argument thoroughly, including its strengths and weaknesses, before worrying about the dramatic touch.

A. PREPARING FOR ORAL ARGUMENT

Preparation is actually a two-step process: study and rehearsal. To be truly ready to stand before a judge and argue your case, you must know your record, your arguments and the authorities they rest on inside and out. Spending sufficient time rereading cases and mastering their facts is essential. This enables you to distinguish adverse precedent without hesitation and to answer confidently the judges' inevitable questions. You need to rehearse, whether in front of a friend, a mirror, or a tape recorder, to become comfortable expressing your arguments orally and to gain a sense of the time needed to express them.

While both kinds of preparation are important, watch out for the trap of spending so much time rehearsing that you fail to master the case. Also, too much rehearsal may make you appear somewhat stale and insincere in your argument. You cannot be "locked into" a certain train of thought and a certain argument when you present your case. You must be ready to be interrupted by the judges and perhaps even side-tracked from the argument you have planned. Your job is to address the judge's concerns and to keep the argument as focused and as much "on-track" as possible. This will also be the first time you will hear your opponents' arguments, and you must be flexible enough to adjust your argument in light of theirs, if the need arises.

What follows is a step-by-step outline of the basic techniques for preparing for oral argument.

1. Study the Record and Authorities. Success in any aspect of oral argument requires complete mastery of the record and briefs before the court. There is no shortcut here. The record and briefs are the basic documents for informing and convincing the court and your job is to know their contents thoroughly. Because the court's decision ultimately turns on the facts, you must have an intimate knowledge of the events giving rise to the cause of action and the facts and issues discussed in the lower court's opinion. Your ability to answer the court's questions with an apt reference to the record will likely enhance the court's confidence in other aspects of your presentation.

You cannot gain an understanding of the record or of the particular facts of cases you cite by relying solely upon your brief or knowledge gained in the process of brief preparation. Oral argument is a separate part of advocacy that requires independent preparation. Indeed, arguments that are not amenable to written presentation may be raised orally before the court (although court rules may restrict the use of cases not cited in the brief), and you may move to correct what judges perceive as flaws in your brief.

You should have a complete understanding of all the cases cited in both sides' briefs. Studying the cases and determining how to analogize to helpful ones and distinguish harmful ones is critically important.

Remember that moot court judges are likely to raise questions about particular cases. To help you study and prepare, you may want to write up short case abstracts and index the record. However, you should become so familiar with the record and relevant cases that you can discuss them without referring to notes.

2. Analyze the Arguments. To devise strategy and choose the arguments to make orally, you need to understand all the issues and arguments arising from the case. Make a methodical attempt to break down the arguments presented in your own and your opponent's briefs. This dissection, along with knowledge of the record and authorities, will give you a complete background against which to make strategic and tactical choices concerning both substance and style.

a. Use your core theory. Long before the argument stage, you developed your "core theory," the one or two sentence explanation of the essence of your case. (Recall the discussion of the core theory in Chapter II, Reading the Record.) Build on this basic framework, embellish the core theory to respond to judge's concerns and explain fully why the court should rule in your favor. Remember that oral argument focuses attention on the most compelling aspects of a case. You may simplify and improve your presentation by choosing arguments that tightly revolve around your case's core theory. In many instances, a powerful argument stresses basically one idea, and comes at that idea from different angles—facts, laws, policy. In organizing your argument, keep in mind the relationship between a particular assertion and the core theory, and decide whether that relationship can be simply and succinctly conveyed orally.

b. Understand specific arguments. Understand the specific arguments made in the briefs, for they will occupy most of your actual argument time. In asserting and attacking these arguments, you will be asked to blend issues with facts and law. Remember that just as in writing the brief, you must argue the facts of your case and explain why existing legal rules should or should not apply.

(1) *Ranking the Arguments' Importance.* As you develop your understanding of the arguments, you should begin to make judgments about the merits of particular points. First, rank arguments in terms of importance to the results desired. Because you have only a short period of time in which to argue, and the time passes far more quickly than you can imagine, you need to decide which arguments are worth emphasizing. There is no single method for making this difficult decision, but some factors to weigh are whether a written argument is too complex to make effectively orally; what policy considerations may move a judge to rule your way; which argument is your "weakest link" and thus likely to be the court's focal concern; which argument is most powerful or convincing; and whether you are arguing with or against current trends in the law. In addition, you must know exactly what

the lower court did and exactly what you seek to have affirmed or reversed. Indeed, one favorite question of moot court judges is simply, "Counsel, what is it that you want me to do here?"

(2) *Evaluating the Arguments' Merits.* You should also identify the strengths and weaknesses of the arguments. Be objective when making this judgment. Take your opponent's arguments seriously. The court will probably confront you with the essence of those arguments, and in many cases the court will present your opponent's positions better than your opponent does.

Be objective about your own arguments as well. The judges will be most likely to object to those points that are the most innovative or lacking in significant case authority. Every argument has a weak point; make sure you are prepared to respond to an attack on your arguments' frailties. You should also be prepared to perhaps concede on an argument or an adverse case. Think about which arguments you can afford to lose prior to your oral argument. Spending valuable time trying to resurrect a clearly "dead" argument will do you no good, and will prevent you from moving on to your better ones.

3. Strategy and Style. One of the best ways to understand what you must do with your oral argument is to understand what you should not do. You should not provide the judges with a jury summation, nor merely recite your brief. You should not debate the case and appear overly confrontational and adverserial. And most important, you should not read your notes as if they were a script.

So what is an oral argument? Most importantly, your argument should be a conversation with the judges. You must be flexible and responsive. To the extent that you may have prepared some comments, you must be ready to throw away those notes so as to be responsive to the judges. Oral argument is your chance to dispel the judges' problems with your case, and you simply cannot predict what those problems will be. But if you are well-prepared and flexible, you will have no trouble addressing any question that they may raise.

The argument should be lively, vivid, and occasionally improvised. If need be, use a clever illustration to make your point clear. Pick up on the judges' metaphors and hypotheticals, and use them to your advantage. Often, nothing is more clear and more persuasive than using an example which the judges can actually picture in their minds, as that image is likely to be remembered far beyond your presentation.

All of this is to say that oral argument is not a rehearsed play, nor is it an oral reincarnation of your brief. A successful argument will be a lively and substantive conversation with the judges. To that end, you should have some understanding of the institutional factors which might influence a judge's attitudes. What arguments are likely to appeal to a particular judge based on ideological predilections? Will the bench be "hot" or "cold"—that is, are the judges likely to have read your brief before your argument? Your predictions as to these factors will be just that—predictions. But you should nevertheless at least think about them, as these factors often will influence the nature of your conversation with the panel.

Similarly, whether your client is appellant or appellee will have great bearing. Appellant speaks first and has the opportunity to choose to raise particular issues and to set the tone of the argument. The appellee, on the other hand, can tailor his argument to the concerns of the court evident in their questions to the appellant. The opportunity for rebuttal gives appellant the last word, but in another sense appellee has the upper hand since appellant seeks to overturn a lower court judgment already entered against him.

4. Prepare Arguments for Oral Presentation. Once you have considered strategic issues and have evaluated the strengths, weaknesses, and relative importance of arguments, you are ready to begin organizing and preparing the arguments you intend to make in court.

Whatever arguments you decide to make, you will need to prepare written notes, even though you may never refer to them during the argument itself. A court will not be impressed if you do not refer to your notes, but a court will disapprove if, once questioned, you are unable to remember your argument. A few brief notes will help you avoid this pitfall.

Preparing written outlines or notes also serves several functions in the process of readying for your argument. Sketching out your arguments may help you to focus and refine them, as well as to commit them to memory. However, abbreviated outlines and catch phrases are probably more useful when you stand up for your argument, as they will allow you to recall at a glance the whole substance of an argument. Remember not to bring a prepared speech with you to the podium. In fact, the procedural rules for the federal appellate courts prohibit the reading of briefs at argument. A prepared speech will do you no good as your conversation with the panel evolves and inevitably differs from what you planned.

Some students decide to write out the first minute (about a page) of their argument. While reading this introduction may make the opening moments easier if you are not used to public speaking, it may erode a judge's confidence in your ability. Write it out, if you must, but leave it behind when you move to the lectern so that you can begin your presentation with your eyes on the judges. By that time, if you have prepared sufficiently, you will be so familiar with your case that you can rely on your instincts to carry you through.

5. Anticipate Questions and Responses. In moot court, judges ask questions incessantly. For the novice advocate, developing the ability to answer questions presents the most formidable challenge. If you carefully anticipate questions and think about answers, you will welcome the judges' inquiries. After all, your role in oral argument is to explain your position, and it will be easier to explain if a judge tells you exactly what troubles him about the case. A lively interchange between judge and advocate is what makes oral argument exhilarating. Time passes much more quickly when you are under fire, and the argument focuses more closely on the issues the judges deem relevant. The judges' questions transform the argument from a staid speech into a dynamic conversation.

From the very beginning of your preparation for oral argument you should be thinking about and jotting down a "question list." Put yourself in the judges' position as you read the record and the briefs. Try to pinpoint factual inconsistencies, expansive readings of the law, and barely distinguishable adverse cases, all of which are likely to arouse a judge's interest. If a case is truly damaging to your argument, do not deny the problem. Rather, recognize the concern raised by that court and address it.

Prepare to answer questions just as you prepared the affirmative arguments. However, always maintain flexibility in developing answers since the judges' questions will inevitably differ somewhat from the ones for which you prepared.

Your ability to answer questions effectively will depend on your understanding of the case and the arguments put forward by both sides. If you have a thorough understanding of the case, you will be able to tailor your responses to judges' questions so as to advance your argument. In the limited amount of time you have, you should not waste any opportunity to further your case. Point out to the judges how each response "fits" into your overall argument and how it supports your core theory. If you are successful in doing this, you will address the issues with which the judges are concerned while proving that they need not be concerned with those issues any longer, as they all actually feed into your argument.

6. Practice Your Argument. Practicing is perhaps the most effective way to improve your argument, both substantively and stylistically. It allows you to practice emphasis, timing, pronunciation, and other delivery techniques, and to grow comfortable using the argument's particular vocabulary. It gives practice in handling questions, and often leads to the formulation of more questions or the substantive improvement of the argument. Finally, it allows you to be sure that the argument is complete, building confidence that will relieve the pressure when you are called to the lectern.

You should practice in live court situations where others can react to the argument and delivery and you can develop a sense of just how long it will take to cover every important point. (Many students are surprised to find that their limited time is up well before they have completed their argument.) A moot court team provides an excellent forum for rehearsal, allowing both the appellant and appellee halves of the team to challenge each other and to develop and practice arguments. The opportunity to confront the strongest opposing arguments in a practice oral argument will make the real argument more cohesive and polished.

Practicing alone before audio or video tape recorders may be less effective for some people, because it does not provide for listener response and may divert attention from the argument to the technology. Reviewing your recorded performance will give you the chance to detect weaknesses in the argument, awkward phrases, hesitations, wordiness, distracting movements, and other flaws in delivery. If no friend or classmate is willing to listen to you rehearse and if recording equipment is unavailable, practice in front of a mirror or in the shower. In general, some rehearsal (even by yourself) is better than none at all.

B. ORGANIZING THE ORAL ARGUMENT

1. Basic Structure of Oral Argument. The decisions you make with regard to framing issues, choosing arguments, and setting the proper tone will probably be made within the context of a fixed structure for your presentation. This section discusses the various elements contained in a traditional oral presentation. You need not use this basic framework in your oral argument; indeed, the appellee's argument, in particular, may as a matter of strategy radically differ from the model. However, most oral presentations do conform, at least roughly, to this framework. As a general rule, you should ask yourself what a judge would like to know first about the case. What manner of presentation would immediately inform the judge of the central issue? What is an interesting, logical, respectful and positive approach? The traditional model is one commonsense approach to answering these questions.

a. The opening statement. The opening statement briefly and succinctly introduces counsel and describes the nature of the case. Counsel introduces himself in a formal yet simple way by giving his name and his relationship to his client. For example:

> May it please the court, my name is Robin Ball. I represent the appellants, Rebecca and Scott Bell-Wesley.

Your initial introduction of the case to the court should combine the necessary facts and legal analysis to describe the nature of the case and enable the judges to focus their experience and understanding on specific issues presented. State the question concisely and present it so as to include your core theory.

An introduction that launches into a contorted description of procedural history or immediately begins reciting facts gives the court inadequate background for the arguments that follow. In either case, avoid confusing openings like these.

> This case comes here on appeal to review a judgment of the Superior Court for the State of Ames which, after rejecting plaintiffs' legal claim, was entered for defendant.

> The facts involve an action by plaintiff for damages resulting from Dr. O'Toole's negligent performance of a vasectomy which led to the wrongful birth of plaintiffs' child.

Be sure to include all the information the court needs to understand your argument. An opening like one of these plunges straight into the facts without letting the court know what questions it must resolve. The court will either lose interest or interrupt. Occasionally moot court judges are forced to pry facts and issues out of students by a kind of cross-examination. This means that the student is neither doing his job nor helping his case.

In this situation, the presentation could have been very simple and clear:

> This case is here on appeal from the Superior Court of Ames. The Bell-Wesleys seek to establish that the defendant's negligent performance of a vasectomy creates an actionable wrongful birth claim. The Bell-Wesleys contend that as a result of Dr. O'Toole's negligence, they should recover damages for lost earnings, the costs of raising their son, Frank, pain and suffering, emotional trauma, and the sacrifice of their chosen lifestyle.

From such an introduction, the court knows at the outset what the questions are, and will listen to the facts with some appreciation of their relevance.

In team situations, the first speaker should introduce both himself and his teammate. The second speaker will repeat her own name before launching into her half of the argument. In addition, the first speaker should outline for the court the issues that each of the advocates will develop. For example:

> I will argue that wrongful birth is actionable as a standard medical malpractice claim. My co-counsel will demonstrate that the Bell-Wesleys are entitled to the types of damages just mentioned. The facts, as found by the Superior Court, are as follows. . ..

This simple device enables the court to organize its own questioning efficiently.

b. Statement of facts. As in the brief, the oral statement of facts sets the stage for resolving legal issues in a specific factual setting. The court wants to know what the circumstances are behind this dispute or controversy, since the court's job is ultimately that of favoring one party over another. Delving into legal issues without telling the court the facts is asking the judge to decide an abstract question of legal principle rather than a specific controversy.

Do not assume that the court knows any of the facts prior to the argument; state every critical fact. Time constraints and strategic choices should prompt you to eliminate all but the most relevant facts. The statement of facts must be framed and delivered to present your point of view and the merits of your client's case. Remember, however, that if your statement of the facts is too slanted or is misleading, you will lose credibility with the court. A carefully organized statement of the facts must present the operative facts fairly.

Practice the statement of facts with someone unfamiliar with the case to see if you are clearly conveying the important information. Because the statement should be as short as possible to achieve the desired goal, succinctness and precision are essential.

In team situations, only the first speaker for each side gives the statement of facts. Therefore, remember to highlight facts important to both partners' arguments. As for the appellee, a complete restatement of the facts is usually unnecessary. If appellee believes that appellant has omitted or mischaracterized particular facts of importance, however, he should mention that to the court.

c. Concise outline of legal arguments. After presenting the facts that suggest the legal questions involved, you should provide a concise outline of the legal argument, akin to your brief's table of contents, where the argument headings double as a summary outline of the entire argument. Having completed the recitation of the facts, the appellant in *Bell-Wesley v. O'Toole* might present her outline in the following manner:

> There are two parts to the argument that the Bell-Wesley's claim for damages should be recognized. First, Dr. O'Toole's behavior contains all the elements of standard medical malpractice. Second, recognizing an exception to standard tort law would contravene public policies favoring family planning and self-determination, discouragement of careless behavior, and the redress of harms. I will discuss in turn each part of the argument.

The summary outline gives the judge a pattern in which to fit later arguments, indicates the order in which matters will be discussed, and enables the court to defer its questions until the appropriate time. Moreover, by announcing an outline near the beginning of your argument—even if in perfunctory form—you at least make the point that these particular arguments are important enough to be raised at oral argument. Even if lengthy questioning on an early point precludes discussing all of the topics on your outline, you have at least raised all of the important points and can summarize each at the conclusion of your argument.

d. The arguments

(1) *Presenting Arguments.*   At the preparation stage you determined which arguments were strongest, most important, and most persuasive. Make sure to put the best points to the court early in the argument. This both attracts the court's attention and ensures that the strongest points are not left out if you get sidetracked by questions. As a general rule, present arguments orally as you did in the brief, using an "inverted pyramid" structure. State conclusions first and then support them with facts and law. Setting out a series of premises and then drawing conclusions is often too complicated to be effective in oral argument.

(2) *Blending Fact and Law.*   All arguments combine law and facts, and finding the appropriate mixture is something you will want to consider in organizing your presentation. Blending facts and law is essential because an argument that discusses black-letter trends since Blackstone's era without mentioning their relevance to the parties in court, or one that describes the endlessly complex contract negotiations between the parties without alluding once to the legal implications of their dispute, is doomed to fail. Unless you integrate the factual and legal elements of your argument, no court will ever be able to understand your position or rule in your favor.

There is no formula for a perfectly blended argument. The relative proportions of fact and law differ in every case. You need to consider your own case closely. Are you asking the court to extend doctrine and create a new rule of law? If so, you may want to concentrate on legal arguments and explain why the existing rule has led to unfair results in prior cases. On the other hand, if you are merely asking the court to apply an established rule of law, you may want to spend more time on your facts.

Remember too that no court will tolerate a fabricated fact or a misrepresentation. Even a slight exaggeration is too much. If the record says "some" patrons of the casino were dancing on the craps table, don't tell the court that "most" of them were unless you are willing to invoke the judges' wrath.

e. Conclusion.
Conclude your oral presentation by summarizing the most important arguments. This is particularly helpful if the court has broken up your arguments with questions. Explain to the court the relationship between each of your arguments, integrating them into an overall framework. Emphasize the strongest arguments in the conclusion.

When there is nothing left to say, thank the court and sit down—even if time is left. Any makeweight argument used to fill up the remaining time is likely to leave the court with an unfavorable impression and could seriously weaken those arguments already made.

2. Appellee's Argument. Since the traditional appellee's argument is structurally similar to that of the appellant, the guidelines listed above will be helpful. If you represent the appellee, listen closely to appellant's argument and to the questions the judges ask. Take notes to remind yourself of points on which the judges dwell. You should have a tentative outline of your argument prepared but you should be ready to revamp and revise it on the spur of the moment in order to respond to issues that obviously concern the judges. You may also decide that something the appellant said during her presentation should be refuted or corrected. In short, be prepared to be spontaneous.

As a general rule, it is best to develop your own case rather than to attack your opponent's. However, on the points where the two sides directly disagree, you cannot avoid talking about the appellant's contentions. In these situations, aggressive appellees may explicitly attack appellant's assertions. This affirmative method brings to the sharp and focused attention of the court the clear distinctions between the two parties.

3. Appellant's Rebuttal. At the beginning of the argument, the appellant may wish to reserve time for rebuttal. Rebuttal time should be used to clarify any prior arguments and react to the appellee's presentation. Because it is the court's last impression of the case, rebuttal can be very important.

Your time for oral argument is very limited, so the time reserved for rebuttal should not be extensive. If you have reserved some time to rebut, remember that you do not have to use the time. In many circumstances, it is most effective to decline the use of rebuttal time— this will indicate to the court that you remain confident in your case, even after the other side has presented its argument, and will avoid the embarrassment of an ill-prepared and rambling rebuttal.

Generally, you should use your rebuttal time only if you have a point to make that will directly contest a point made by the appellee. You should be short, crisp, and clear in your rebuttal. Make your point, and then end the argument. If you decide to use your reserved time and find yourself at a loss for words, keep in mind that the court often will have little trouble taking advantage of the opportunity to question you some more about your initial argument. Therefore, be very wary of rebuttals. They can be very effective, but they can also give the judges that perfect opportunity to re-attack your argument.

C. QUESTIONS BY THE COURT

1. The Value of Questions. Questions from the court reveal to you what the judge is thinking. You finally learn whether the court understands your ideas, whether the judge agrees with your framing of the issues, and what troubles the judge.

Listening to the question makes the task of persuasion easier. If it is apparent from the nods of the judges or from their questions that they fully agree with the position taken on an issue, it may be a good idea to shorten the scheduled presentation and move on to a new area. If the questions indicate the court disagrees with certain contentions, it may be wise to amplify and present even more persuasively reasons that might convince the court of the position's validity. In short, the questions will allow you to tailor the argument to the court's reaction.

Be aware at all times that not every question asked is an attack on your position; some questions are designed to support your view and some are simply points about which the judge is confused and has no preconceived opinion.

2. Effective Answering

   a. Be responsive. Using the court's own questions to persuade it of the soundness of a contention requires responsiveness on your part. To respond to questions adequately, you must understand what the judge has asked. Always listen carefully. If the question is unclear, you may properly ask the judge to repeat or rephrase it. If the implications of a question are unclear, you may repeat what you understand the judge to be asking and inquire whether that is what the judge means. You want to clarify your position and you need to clarify puzzling questions in order to do so. It is often wise to pause before you begin to speak to reflect briefly on the question. Taking a few seconds to collect your thoughts usually results in a more focused response. It is far more effective to pause and organize your response than to attempt one that is prompt, yet unclear.

A judge's questions may spring from confusion, misunderstanding, concern about the consequences of broadening a legal rule, hostility born of a personal conviction that your position is wrong, or a genuine desire to help you regain your footing after tough interrogation from a less than friendly colleague. You need to listen closely to questions to ascertain what troubles a judge and why. Your answers must explain and clarify your position until you satisfy the judge; if you try to move on without meeting her concerns, she will badger you until you do. If the judge believes you are being evasive, she may grow exasperated and simply decide to rule against you.

If the judge tries to corner you into a "yes" or "no" response to a particular question that you feel would be inadequate, provide the one-word response but quickly follow-up with a further explication of why your position is not so clear-cut. Always be respectful, courteous, and above all, responsive. Under no circumstances should you tell a judge that you will get to her question later, when you have finished the point you are making. You must tailor your tentative schedule to fit the judges' interests, and an unwillingness to answer a question when put signals disrespect.

Recognize and accept friendly questions from a judge, the type of question that frames the argument for you or otherwise moves your position along. These types of questions often come when another member of the panel has questioned you intensively. Inexperienced counsel have more than once refused an argument set out on a silver platter by a judge who restated counsel's argument in a new way or supported his position with a new argument.

Be prepared to answer the hardest questions, since the court's decision will often turn on them. Almost any question can be antici-pated and hence answered if you take the time to think through the problems and implications of the question of your case. At the same time, you must remember that a judge's question may not be the one you anticipated. Tailor your answer accordingly; a judge likes to think that her question is unique and will probably resent what sounds like a "pat" answer.

b. Advocate. Use your responses to advance your argument, even if that means departing from the order your outline sets out. Once the court seems satisfied with an answer, try to make a smooth transition from that response to another, related topic. Your argument will be more effective if it flows naturally from one point to another. Do all you can to maintain the argument's continuity and avoid a moment of awkward silence when the judges have concluded a line of questioning and await your next set of points.

Using a question as a vehicle to advance a line of argument is not an easy skill to learn, but here is an example of how someone arguing for the appellant in *Bell-Wesley v. O'Toole* might go about it. If a judge asked, "Why didn't the Bell-Wesleys give the child up for adoption?", the appellants' attorney might answer:

> 1. Your honor, it may seem logical merely to give up the child for adoption and thus mitigate any of the expenses associated with the child which are requested in this action as damages. 2. However, the courts, and indeed society, recognize the special relationship created between a parent and child. Very rarely do we ever ask a parent to give up a child. And this occurs only when the parents are incapable of caring for the child. 3. Indeed, your honor, it is because of this social and moral ethic which links a child to his or her natural parents that there are substantial damages in this action. A child, while unexpected, should and

must not be taken away. Nevertheless, the unexpected costs associated with the child incurred through negligence should be borne by Dr. O'Toole, the perpetrator of the negligent acts.

Part 1 of the sample answer restates the question. By restating the question counsel has shown that she fully understands the question asked. (Indeed, the judge could have interrupted and corrected any misperception of the question.) Moreover, she has also used the opportunity to add the context of damages to an otherwise open-ended and unmanageable question regarding adoption. This move takes a step toward creating not just a responsive answer, but one which affirmatively advances the argument. In Part 2, counsel has directly responded to the question. In Part 3, she uses the question and answer as a platform to advance her argument that extensive damages ought to be awarded. The attorney moves from a responsive position ("The Bell-Wesleys shouldn't have to give the child up for adoption, because . . ."), to an affirmative one ("Because the child shouldn't be given up for adoption, therefore. . .").

Good preparation is the key to answering questions. Although you may feel unprepared and apprehensive going into your first oral argument, you will probably be pleasantly surprised at how much you actually know and how well you do. One final point: if you truly cannot think of an answer, be very honest with the court. Being evasive is more detrimental than simply saying, "I don't know."

3. Particular Types of Questions Judges Might Ask

a. Questions seeking information about the facts. If the statement of facts is adequate and gives the court some idea of which facts were crucial, many time-consuming questions may be avoided. If factual items are central, a judge will often want to read them directly from the record. Consequently, you should be prepared to answer such questions with a reference to the page in the record where the fact can be found. You should also be aware of the possible relevance of facts that are absent from the record. Judges are likely to ask you about these missing facts.

Questions about the facts may also come from the judge who feels that you have wandered too far from the facts of the case into an abstract discourse on the law. You may well want to respond to these questions by sticking a little more closely in the argument to the case's factual setting. This involves wording arguments to bring out the facts of the case. For instance, in making an argument concerning plaintiff's reliance on a statement by the defendant, counsel might say, "Mr. Goldstein relied on Ms. Wolfe's statement that the shipment of volleyballs arrived on time," rather than dryly saying, "Reliance by the plaintiff is indicated in this case."

b. Questions about "policy considerations." Questions of this nature are often phrased like this: "Counsel, would you comment upon . . .." Here the court wants to hear a fuller exposition of the factors that you deem relevant to a decision, and possibly a countering of opposing policy considerations. The question will usually point up something that is troubling the judge. Your job is to find ways to recast and supplement points covered in the briefs, so as to allay the court's concerns.

Sometimes, questions of this sort are phrased more argumentatively: "But, counsel, isn't it clear that . . .." The form of the question does not mean that the judge has necessarily decided against the position advanced. It may well be that her thinking is currently adverse to that position. Yet you should not give up but rather try to put the point in a new light and use the utmost persuasion to change her mind.

c. Questions directed at the authorities cited. When a judge asks about a cited case, she wants something more than a dry recitation of the facts and the holding. She wants to know how it relates to the case being argued. Does it constitute binding precedent on the point (not likely in a mythical jurisdiction where every issue is one of first impression), or does it show the existing framework of law into which the desired result must be fitted? Above all, the judge wants to know why the earlier court decided as it did. What considerations controlled the decision? Has the weight to be given these factors changed since the court decided the earlier case?

You may have to argue against what seems to be established precedent. If this is the case, a frontal attack is usually appropriate. However, the precedent may actually be inapposite in the circumstances of the case before the court. When overturning established precedent is likely to be the primary subject for conversation between you and the judges, the following questions may be important:

(1) Is the precedent grounded on sound public policy?

(2) Is the precedent working well or badly in practice?

(3) Is the precedent being followed universally?

(4) Will the precedent become less useful in the future?

(5) Will the precedent create injustice in this particular case?

(6) Is the precedent consistent with trends in similar areas of law?

(7) Can a valid and consistent exception to the precedent be made without detracting from the force of the precedent as a whole?

d. Questions directed at particular legal arguments. Questions of this type test an argument's logic. Loose statements of holdings, overbroad analogies, and imprecise wording can unleash a veritable barrage of questions about the mechanics of your arguments.

Some questions are inevitable in that they naturally spring from the arguments' complexity or implications. These questions test your mastery of the case and depth of understanding of the surrounding law. Judges often want to know how far an argument will take the court down an uncharted path. These questions require line drawing, yet this is precisely where the court needs guidance. If a judge is persuaded that a distinction can be drawn between the case at bar and a future case where the doctrine espoused seems applicable but where the result is untenable, then she is well on the way to adopting a favorable result. If you want to prevent the application of the doctrine espoused, be prepared to deliver what is often called a "parade of horribles," the negative implications of accepting opposing counsel's line of argument. Think through the implications of doctrines advocated by your opponent in order to be ready to offer responsive answers that may help the court decide the case.

Keep in mind that the case being argued involves specific parties in a single fact situation. If you weave the facts neatly into your answers, you can probably avoid getting trapped into defending a broad general principle against all possible attacks.

4. Questioning in Team Situations. Although judges in moot court competition will ordinarily refrain from questioning one member of the team about issues for which the other member was primarily responsible, it is advisable for each co-counsel to understand the basic arguments of the case. If questioning becomes too specific, ask the court either to permit your co-counsel to return to the lectern or, if you are the first oralist, to await your teammate's later appearance. If properly prepared, the second speaker may also take the opportunity to cover crucial points that his co-counsel inadvertently omitted and to develop further any answers that may have been inadequate.

D. PRESENTING THE ORAL ARGUMENT

1. Be Yourself. If there is one general rule of presenting an argument, it is "Be yourself." If you are ordinarily even-tempered and soft spoken, don't plan to impress the court with a flashy, fist-pounding display of rhetoric. Don't try to fit yourself into someone else's mold. There is no single right way to argue a case, and the more comfortable you are, the more effective your argument is likely to be.

2. Effective Delivery. Read only if absolutely necessary. A paper barrier between court and counsel inhibits effective presentation. The best advocates have a thorough knowledge of relevant materials. This does not mean that you should become primarily a case-citer. Rather, you should be able to deal quickly and surely with the issues, calling forth relevant arguments without fumbling through a mound of written materials for that case which is "here somewhere," or which "I saw just a moment ago." Eye contact with the judges is helpful and can only be maintained if you have acquired a thorough knowledge of the material you will use in argument.

Quoting cases to support your arguments is sometimes useful, but keep the quotes short and do not use them too often. In general, paraphrasing the language of cases you cited in your brief will be a more effective way of communicating their essence to the judges.

Apply the fundamentals of good public speaking. Avoid orating; an appellate court is not a jury. Avoid legalese and other jargon. Jargon will not impress the judges and even worse, it may distract their attention. Your oral argument should be a conversation with the court, not a speech to it. To some extent the conversational character of your presentation will depend on whether your court asks numerous questions. But even if the judges remain quiet, you should not appear as if you are lecturing the court. Some general points of public speaking to keep in mind are:

- Be heard.
- Use proper emphasis. Avoid a sing-song pattern where your voice goes up and down without emphasizing the proper words.
- Avoid mumbling.
- Use the pause. This device, when used sparingly and judiciously, serves to stress the points being made and helps to regain a judge's attention when he has become preoccupied with a cited passage in the record or brief.
- Maintain eye contact—don't read.

3. What to Take to Court. Given the limited amount of time allotted for oral argument and the need for continuous presentation and dialogue, your ability to refer to materials is limited. Proper preparation will reduce the need to search through materials for your answers.

Take the record and briefs with you to the lectern. The court is more than likely to ask questions that specifically refer to these documents. (Make sure that you tab or clip pertinent pages in the record and briefs so that you can refer to them effortlessly should the need arise.) Two other kinds of materials may be helpful. First, a short outline of points to be covered serves as a helpful checklist to jog your memory. Second, note cards containing important facts and quotations may be useful. You can write key words pertaining to particular points or cases on separate cards, which can be shuffled discreetly during your presentation.

4. Attitude Toward the Court. Your attitude toward the court should be one of respectful equality. You are not servile to the court, but you must accord judges due respect. Even in the heat of hard questioning, you must take care to be receptive, cooperative and in no way show annoyance at the trend of the questioning. Give definite answers to the court's questions and be aggressive with the material even as you avoid being aggressive in manner.

5. Handling Miscitations and Misrepresentations by Opposing Counsel. Bring any miscitations and misrepresentations of opposing counsel to the court's attention only if you feel they are important to the case. In evaluating their importance, you should determine whether they may be influencing an essential argument, or whether, without help, the court will be unable to find the appropriate citation. In addition, it is important to evaluate whether the court realizes that the material has been misrepresented. However, remember not to appear to be attacking opposing counsel personally.

6. Formal Conduct. A few customs of formal conduct should be observed in the oral argument. The customs do not vary much from courtroom to courtroom. When beginning the argument, rise and say, "May it please the court," or "If the court please," and introduce yourself. In answering questions, address the judge as "Your Honor." In referring to members of the court, "Judge Smith" or "The Chief Justice" is appropriate. Opposing counsel should be referred to as such, or as "Ms. Overton" or "counsel for the defendant" but never as "my opponent." Associate counsel is called "my colleague," "my associate," or "Ms. Phethean."

Appendix

GENERAL RULES OF STYLE AND CITATION OF AUTHORITIES

The questions of why and when to cite authorities in a brief have already been discussed. This appendix is designed to indicate the functions that the form of citation serves and to suggest the basic rules governing form. These rules are based on *A Uniform System of Citation* (14th ed. 1986), published by the Harvard Law Review Association, subject to modification where brief writing citation requirements differ from the needs of other types of legal work. That book (commonly called the "bluebook"), which contains rules governing matters not covered in this appendix, is an extremely useful reference work. The rules in this appendix are current as of December, 1990. For areas not covered herein, the reader should consult the bluebook itself.

Rules presented in this chapter pertain directly to citations in briefs. Citations to authority are placed in the text of the brief and are not put in footnote form.

This chapter deals in Part A with the general rules that govern the writing of a brief. The remaining parts of the chapter deal with the technicalities relating to the citation of authorities in the brief. Part B takes up the necessary elements of information which a citation must contain. Part C deals with the indication of the purpose and weight of citations, and the treatment of multiple authorities cited for the same point. (The actual form of citations is dealt with in Part D (Cases), Part E (Statutes and Constitutions), and Part F (Secondary Authorities).)

For the most part, citations in this chapter are only illustrative of proper form. They do not refer to actual cases.

A. GENERAL RULES OF STYLE

1. ABBREVIATIONS

Many abbreviations permitted in citations are not acceptable when used in the body of the brief or in the Table of Citations. For a list of abbreviations in case names, see Part D.1.c of this section or the bluebook.

Well-known statutes and agencies may be designated by initials after the full name has been written out once. The periods are omitted unless the initials designate a case reporter. "The National Labor Relations Board has done commendable work. At its inception, the

NLRB was not. . . ." Names of states and the "United States" must not be abbreviated.

2. CAPITALIZATION

a. Capitalization of Specific Words. The following words are capitalized only in the following situations:

- "Act"—when referring to a specific act: the National Labor Relations Act . . . the Act.
- "Circuit"—when used with the circuit number. First Circuit.
- "Code"—when referring to a specific code: the 1939 and 1954 Codes.
- "Constitution"—when referring to the United States Constitution or to any constitution in full. Exception: federal constitution. Amendments to the Constitution and the "Bill of Rights" are capitalized, but articles are left in lowercase.
- "Court"—when naming any court in full; otherwise, only when referring to the United States Supreme Court: the Supreme Court of Illinois; the [state] supreme court; the court of appeals; the Court of Appeals for the Fifth Circuit.
- "Federal"—only when the word it modifies is capitalized.
- "Justice"—when referring to a Justice of the United States Supreme Court.
- "Rule"—when part of a proper name given in full.
- "State"—when the word it modifies is capitalized.
- "Statute"—when part of a proper name given in full.

b. Capitalization of Famous Old Statutes and Rules. The names of famous old statutes and rules such as the Statute of Frauds and the Rule Against Perpetuities are customarily capitalized. The statute of limitations is not capitalized.

c. Words Denoting Groups or Officeholders. These (such as the Congress, the Senate, the Agency, the Commission, the President) are capitalized when referring to a specific federal government body, office, or official. Adjectival forms of these words are not capitalized (congressional hearing, the agency hearing, etc.)

3. ITALICIZATION AND UNDERLINING

Italicization is indicated on a typewriter by underlining and is used in the following circumstances:

a. Case Names. The names of both parties and the "v." between should be underlined. Italicization is used also in abbreviated references to cases. "The *Jones* case held. . . ." The Latin words in a case name are also underlined. *In re McLaughlin; Ex parte Savin.*

b. Introductory Signals. All introductory signals are italicized.

c. Foreign Words and Phrases. Italicization of foreign words and phrases is determined by the word's incorporation into common English usage. The second edition of *Merriam-Webster New International Dictionary* is an excellent source for making this determination. Words to be italicized are indicated in that work (and its abridged editions) by a prefix of two vertical parallel bars.

> *(1) Foreign words always italicized: ex parte, ex rel., i.e., in re, inter alia, inter se, passim, quaere, semble, sic., sub nom.,* and *supra.*

> *(2) Foreign words not italicized include:* ad hoc, a fortiori, amicus curiae, bona fide, certiorari, de novo, dictum, ipso facto, mandamus, per curiam, per se, prima facie, pro rata, quo warranto, res judicata, stare decisis, and subpoena (and its modifiers).

4. NUMBERS, SYMBOLS, AND DATES

Numbers under 100 should always be written out in the body of a brief, except when relating to a statistical study, or when used in a date. The month of a date should always be written out.

The word "section" must be spelled out, unless part of a citation. The symbols for dollar ($) and percent (%) should only appear with numerals, but a symbol should never begin a sentence. If numerals are not used in a sentence, the words "dollar" and "percent" must be spelled out.

5. QUOTATIONS

Quotations under 50 words in length, set off by quotation marks, are incorporated in the regular flow of the text. Those more than 50 words in length must be indented and single spaced. Indented quotations are not set off by quotation marks.

a. Placement of Quotation Marks. Periods and commas should always be placed inside quotation marks. All other punctuation marks should be placed outside the quotation marks unless they are part of the material quoted.

b. Omissions From Quotations. Omission of material from a quotation must be indicated. All omissions of material from sentences must be indicated, as well as omissions of sentences and paragraphs from quotations. Sentences and paragraphs are not "omitted" unless they originally fell *within* the quoted material.

(1) Short quotations.   Omission of matter before or after a quotation of a phrase or less need not be indicated, unless it would be misleading to not indicate the omission.

(2) Clarification of noun, pronoun or verb.   When a bracket insertion clarifies a noun or pronoun or changes the tense or number of a verb, the corresponding omission need not be indicated.

(3) Omission at the beginning of a sentence.   The omission of language at the beginning of a quoted sentence is indicated by capitalizing and placing in brackets the first letter of the first word of the quoted section.

(4) Omission of the middle of a sentence.   Omitting language from the middle of a sentence is indicated by inserting three spaced periods set off by a space before the first period and after the last period.

(5) Omission at the end of a sentence.   Omitting language at the end of a sentence is indicated by inserting four spaced periods set off by a space before the first period.

(6) Omission from the middle of a quotation.   The omission of language after the end of a quoted sentence followed by the rest of the quotation is indicated by retaining the period at the end of the quoted sentence and inserting three spaced periods set off by a space before the first period and after the last period.   If the omission is from the start of a new quoted paragraph, the spaced periods are indented.   When an entire paragraph is omitted, four spaced and indented periods are placed where the paragraph would have been.

c. **Alterations in Quotations**

(1) Added italics or omitted footnotes.   Alterations of the quotation, such as the addition of italics to some portion of it or the omission of footnotes are indicated by comments in parentheses at the end of the quotation's citation, and should read: "(emphasis added)" or "(footnotes omitted)."

(2) Change of letter.   A change in a quotation from a lower case letter to a capital is indicated by bracketing the letter.

(3) Supplementary or explanatory words.   Supplementary or explanatory words inserted in a quotation must be enclosed in brackets.   (On typewriters without bracket symbols, brackets may be made with the slash bar and the underlining bar.)

d. **Page Numbers of Quoted Materials.**   Indicate the page upon which a quotation begins and, if it continues to another page, the page on which it ends.   This may be done in the sentence introducing the quoted material.   With a short quotation, the citation may appear as a sentence following the quotation.   Where there is a lengthy, single-spaced, and indented quotation, the citation may appear at the end of the quotation. Preferred practice puts the citation within parentheses if the citation follows an indented quotation. The citation need not be put in parentheses if it appears as the first nonindented material after the indented quotation.

6. TECHNICAL WORDS OF REFERENCE

a. "Infra" and "Ibid." In briefs, use "*id.*" to cite to the immediately preceding authority. Do not use "*infra.*"

b. "Supra." *Supra* is only appropriate for material other than cases or statutes. It is used only when the complete citation of the material appeared previously in the same general discussion. *Introduction to Advocacy, supra.* If necessary to refer to a particular page of a citation previously given in the same general discussion, use the following form: *Introduction to Advocacy, supra* at 35.

c. References to the Record. References to the record of a case should follow the cited material with the letter "R." and the page number in parentheses as (R. 17). This is not underlined.

d. References to Footnotes. References to footnotes in a work are made by using the letter "n." *E.g.,* 1 S. Williston, *Sales* 63 n. 7, 64 nn. 9–11 (rev. ed. 1948).

e. References to Briefs. References to the briefs in a case should appear as follows: Brief for Appellee at 20; Brief for Plaintiff at 7.

7. THE TABLE OF CITATIONS

a. Citation of Cases. The rules of style for citation of cases in the body of the brief also apply in the Table of Citations section. The names of cases are underlined in the Table of Citations section just as they are in the body. The cases are listed in alphabetical order. For examples of proper citation form for a typewritten brief, see the tables of citation in the sample briefs in *Bell-Wesley v. O'Toole* at pp. 62 and 83.

b. Citation of Statutes

(1) Abbreviations. Statute names should be written out more completely in the Table of Citations section. In the body, greater abbreviation is permitted. Maine Revised Statutes ch. 2, § 1 (1930).

(2) Location. Remember that statutes are primary authorities and should be listed immediately following cases in the Table of Citations section.

c. Citations of Secondary Authorities. All secondary authorities are grouped under the heading "Miscellaneous" in the Table of Citations. They should be listed here in alphabetical order.

8. A NOTE ON THE SPACING OF CITATIONS

There are many different rules concerning the spacing of citations in legal materials. Courts, publishers, law firms, law reviews, and other legal writers may follow different schemes, and may even be inconsistent within any one document. This internal inconsistency is to be avoided.

A Uniform System of Citation (13th ed. 1981) suggests a system which is followed in the sample briefs in *Bell-Wesley v. O'Toole.* Single capitals are closed up, *except* when an entity is abbreviated by widely recognized initials and combination of those initials with others would be confusing. *E.g.,* Yale L.J.; Nw. U.L. R.; *But:* U.C.L.A. L. Rev.

For the purposes of these rules, individual numbers are treated as single capitals. *E.g.,* F.2d; N.W.2d; N.Y.S.2d; *But:* So. 2d; Cal. 2d.

Because of the nature of printing process, the typewritten briefs in this book should be consulted for the spacing of citations, rather than the text. They begin on p. 62.

B. NECESSARY ELEMENTS OF INFORMATION

Citations must convey certain essential information. They must (1) identify the authority, (2) indicate where it is found, (3) indicate the "author" of the authority, (4) indicate the date of the authority, and (5) indicate the purpose for which the authority is cited and the weight to be attached to it.

1. IDENTIFICATION OF AUTHORITY

The case name must be stated. Where several different cases are decided with one opinion, or the case name is unusually long, see Part D.1. of this chapter for the proper way of giving this essential information in the briefest form.

2. WHERE THE AUTHORITY MAY BE FOUND

The "location" of the authority is the publication in which it has been printed. When the authority is a judicial decision, it is customary to refer to both the official and the unofficial reporters, if they are available; an exception to this rule exists where the case is decided by the Supreme Court of the United States or by lower federal courts. Both volume and page numbers are necessary.

If the authority is an article, the volume of the periodical in which it appears and the number of the page on which it begins are necessary.

A treatise citation should contain the volume, section and sometimes the topic in which it can be found. Other books are cited similarly except that the author's name and page number are used.

3. INDICATION OF "AUTHOR"

Counsel must indicate the person or persons who wrote or stand behind the printed words on which he relies. If it is a case, the citation must identify precisely the court by which it was decided. This will usually be accomplished by reference to the official reporter in which the opinion appears, since most official reporters cover only the highest court of the state. For instance, *Snow v. Wragg,* 303 Mass. 264, 131 N.E. 206 (1900), shows that the Supreme Judicial Court of Massachusetts decided the case, for it is the only court reported in the Massachusetts Reports. However, some official reporters cover more than the highest court. Almost all unofficial reporters cover more than one court. If the case is in one of this class of reporters, the court must be indicated in parentheses. If the identity of the court is obvious from name of the reporter, the court of decision need not be indicated even if it is not the highest court in the jurisdiction. Thus: *Van Allen v. Semmi,* 24 App. Div. 2d 316, 217 N.Y.S.2d 408 (1965) but *Muir v. Alsup,* 221 Misc. 498, 50 N.Y.S.2d 897 (Sup. Ct. 1944).

If the authority is a treatise, the author must be given. With such authorities as the *American Law of Property,* it is customary to name the editor in parentheses. For more exact information, see the section dealing with citations to secondary authorities (Part F *infra*).

4. DATE

The year in which the case was decided, the article written, the statute enacted, or the treatise published must be given. It may have a direct bearing on the weight which the court will attach to the authority since social conditions or policy may well have changed since that time.

5. INDICATION OF PURPOSE AND WEIGHT OF THE CITATION

It is extremely important to inform the court, through the citation form, of the citation's purpose and to indicate what importance (weight) is to be attached to it. This is accomplished through the use of introductory signals and parenthetical information.

The absence of signal before a citation indicates to the court that the authority cited directly upholds the proposition for which it is cited. It is imperative that counsel master the various signals.

Information as to the weight of the authority is given by the presence or absence of explanatory remarks in parentheses after the case. If one uses a case where the court gave its view on an issue, even though it was not necessary for decision, then he must inform the court that it is dictum. Thus: *Passman v. Anderson,* 343 N.Y. 204, 126 N.E. 675 (1959) (dictum). The explanatory comment in parentheses after the case may contain various other desirable comments such as an indication of the judge who wrote the opinion. Absence of any explanatory data affirmatively indicates certain information to the court. For a more complete discussion, see the section dealing with parentheticals indicating weight (Part C.3. *infra*).

C. INDICATION OF PURPOSE AND WEIGHT; ORDER FOR MULTIPLE AUTHORITIES

Proper citation of all authorities (cases, treatises, statutes, etc.) involves indicating the purpose of the citation through its form—that is, informing the judge of the logical relationship which the cited authority bears to the proposition advanced (support, contradiction, etc.). The citation must also inform the judge of the weight which is to be attached to the authority—that is, whether it is holding, dictum or concurring opinion, etc.

Below is a description of some of the relationships of citation to text which can be indicated by the presence or absence of introductory signals and by the use of particular signals.

Groups of citations are given in "sentences." A new sentence of citations is introduced with a capitalized, introductory signal even though the sentence may contain more than one signal. Within a sentence each citation except the last is followed by a semicolon. The last one is followed by a period. All authorities supporting a point are placed in the same sentence. Authorities opposing the point are placed in a separate one. The authorities and signals are placed in the order listed below. Signals which are capitalized even when they do not begin a sentence are indicated below; all signals must be italicized unless a typewriter is used, in which case they must be underlined.

1. SIGNALS INDICATING PURPOSE

a. Authorities Supporting the Point. When authorities support the proposition advanced, various degrees of support are indicated by the absence of any express signal and by the use of *"e.g.," "accord," "see," "see also,"* and *"cf."*

(1) *[No signal]* No express signal is used when the case directly holds the proposition of law for which it is cited. The absence of an express signal indicates that it is a holding, or identifies the source of a quotation.

(2) *"E.g.,"* Use *"e.g.,"* when there are more examples other than the ones cited but citation to them would not be helpful. This signal should be preceded by a comma when used in

combination with other signals and is always followed by a comma. *E.g., Howarth v. Rice,* 408 F.2d 246 (2d Cir. 1969). *See, e.g., Gould v. Smith,* 212 Mass. 17, 218 N.E.2d 842 (1965).

(3) "Accord," "Accord," may be used when the cited authority directly supports the statement in the text, but in a slightly different way than the authority first cited. Its use is most appropriate when the cases are directly in point but the text quotes from or states the facts of one of the cases. Similarly, the law of one jurisdiction may be cited as in accord with that of another jurisdiction if the law is exactly the same. *Accord, Maguire v. McCurdy,* 325 U.S. 6 (1945). Or, after the principal case: *Bordwin v. Ames,* 98 U.S. 64 (1878); *accord, Chase v. Freeman,* 300 U.S. 27 (1937). Note that *"accord,"* is always followed by a comma.

(4) "See" "See" indicates that the asserted opinion or conclusion will be suggested by an examination of the cited authority rather than that the opinion or conclusion is stated by the authority. *See Gordon v. Cushing,* 251 F.2d 8 (3d Cir.1955).

(5) "See also" Use *"see also"* to cite additional cases that directly support a point when the main case has already been discussed. Follow the citation with a parenthetical explanation of the material's relevance. *See also Roberts v. Stern,* 234 F. 12 (D.C. Cir. 1938); *LeClair v. Presser,* 84 Or. 714, 402 P.2d 102 (1965).

(6) "Cf." If the cited case or other source material expresses a proposition which is only analogous to the point under discussion, but lends some support to the statement, conclusion, or opinion in the brief, use *"cf."* before the citation. *Cf. Smith v. Abrams,* 162 Mo. 220, 140 S.W. 518 (1925).

b. Authorities Opposing the Point. When authorities oppose the proposition advanced, various degrees of opposition are indicated by the use of *"Contra," "But see"* and *"But cf."*

(1) "Contra," Precede the citation with *"Contra,"* when citing cases holding the opposite of a proposition. *"Contra,"* is followed by a comma. This is comparable to when "[no signal]" would be used for support. This signal always begins a new sentence. *Contra, Areeda v. Steiner,* 243 U.S. 21 (1917).

(2) "But see" and "But cf." The citation *"But see"* precedes a case not squarely contradictory to the proposition, but which casts doubt upon it. If the case is only analogous, use *"But cf."* *"But see"* and *"But cf."* are analogous to *"see"* and *"cf."* After the first citation to an authority which opposes the proposition being advanced, the *"But"* is dropped from all the "opposing citation" signals which follow in that sentence. *But see Wilson v. Lodge,* 245 U.S. 18 (1918); *cf. Roosevelt v. Taft,* 300 U.S. 200

(1940). Note that these signals always begin a new sentence unless the first signal is *"contra."*

c. Authority Not Lending Support to Proposition. When the cited authority is broader in scope than, or develops a question analogous to, discussion in text without lending support to the proposition asserted, *"see generally"* indicates the cited authority can be profitably compared with the proposition. As with other signals, a parenthetical explanation helps the reader understand the case's relevance. *See generally* Brylawski, *Welfare Systems and Poverty in the United States,* 68 Yale L.J. 812 (1966). *"See generally"* always begins a new sentence of citations.

d. Comparing Authorities With One Another. To compare one cited case with another case, rather than with the text of the brief, use *"Compare . . . with. . . ."* *Compare Vogel v. Stroh,* 205 F.2d 811 (2d Cir. 1959), *with Britton v. Buchanan,* 204 F.2d 367 (3d Cir. 1959).

2. ORDER OF AUTHORITIES

Multiple authorities on the same point must be cited in the order explained below. However, it is seldom wise to give more than two or three authorities for a particular point, especially in moot court competition.

a. Order of Signals. In a citation string, citations are grouped in an order dependent upon the introductory signal preceding them. Each signal or absence of a signal applies to all citations following it until another signal is given or the sentence ends. Signals are given in the order in which they are described in the preceding section, that is, with citations preceded by no signal coming first, signals indicating support next, all signals indicating opposition next, and other signal types following. A sentence only contains authority that is either supporting, opposing or neither. If both supporting and opposing citations are used, two sentences must be used. Within a multiple citation of authorities on the same point, signal groups are given in the following order:

(1) Holding (no signal) (2) *e.g.,* (3) *accord,* (4) *see* (5) *see also* (6) *cf.* (7) *Contra,* (8) *But see* (9) *But cf.* (10) *See generally*

Note the use of citation sentences in the following example. Fed. R. Civ. P. 9(a); *accord,* N.J.R. Civ. P. 9(a); *see Ehrlich v. Grossman,* 215 N.E.2d 919 (Mass. 1966); *cf.* N.Y.R. Civ. Prac. 97 (McKinney 1962). *Contra, Arp. v. Grenier,* 234 F.2d 425 (5th Cir. 1956) (rule 9(a) invalid); *see* 2 J. Moore, *Federal Practice* ¶ 9.02 (2d ed. 1948); *cf.* Iowa R. Civ. P. 101. *See generally Filvoroff v. Wertheimer,* [1953] 1 Q.B. 646.

b. Order Within Signals. Within each introductory signal group, cases are given first, statutes second, and secondary authority last. Specific order within these groups is given below.

(1) Cases. Counsel should first cite the strongest authority by the most persuasive court. All other things being equal, cases are arranged according to the courts issuing the cited opinion (prior history, etc., is irrelevant to the order). All the United States courts of appeals are treated as one court for this purpose, as are all district courts. Within each court, order is given chronologically, with the most recent decisions first.

Federal:

- United States Supreme Court decisions.
- courts of appeals.
- district courts.
- other federal courts.
- administrative agencies.

State:

- state court decisions (in alphabetical order of states, then by rank of court within the state).
- state agencies (in alphabetical order of states, then alphabetically within each state).

Foreign:

- foreign courts, common law followed by civil-law (in alphabetical order of countries, then by rank of court within each country).

Note: Within groups of cases preceded by the same introductory signal, all citations to holdings precede all citations to (1) alternative holdings, (2) concurring or dissenting opinions, and (3) dicta. These latter three classifications are treated as a single group and no special order among them is required.

(2) Statutes and Constitutions. Subject to the rule that the strongest authority should be cited first the following order should be used:

    (a) Constitutions (U.S. and then alphabetically by state)

    (b) Federal statutes

        i   currently in force, in order of U.S.C. title

        ii currently in force but not in U.S.C. (most recent first)

        iii rules of evidence and procedure

        iv repealed statutes

  (c) State statutes (alphabetically by state)

     i   in current codification

     ii   currently in force, but not in current codification (most recent first)

     iii rules of evidence and procedure

     iv repealed statutes (most recent first)

  (d) Foreign statutes (alphabetically by jurisdiction)

     i   currently in force

     ii   repealed

  (e) Municipal ordinances, etc.

Note: Although statutes usually follow cases in a multiple citation, an exception is made when a statute and a case construing it are cited. Where a case construes a statute the two citations should be separated by *"construed in":* Ind. Code § 475 (Burns' Ann. 1934), *construed in Hoffman v. State,* 75 Ind. 918, 38 N.E.2d 475 (1945).

(3) Secondary Materials. Within each of the following categories, citations are listed alphabetically by author or, if the author is unknown, by title.

  (a) Books

  (b) Articles

  (c) Student written law review material (listed alphabetically by periodical)

  (d) signed book reviews

  (e) student-written book notes

  (f) newspapers

  (g) annotations

  (h) unpublished materials

3. PARENTHETICALS INDICATING WEIGHT AND EXPLANATION

a. Parentheticals Indicating Weight. When a case is cited for material other than a clear non-alternative majority holding, indicate this in parentheses after the date of the case. Thus, (1) dicta, (2) concurring or dissenting opinions, (3) points decided by implication, (4) plurality opinions, and (5) points on which the holding of the court is not clear must be so indicated.

(1) Dicta. If the proposition was not necessary to the decision in that case, it is dictum; this fact must be conveyed. This information is shown by proceeding as follows:

  (a) Place the word "dictum" in parentheses at the end of the citation.

(b) List the page on which the dictum appears in both the official and unofficial reporter, as well as the page on which the case begins. *Frederick v. Schwarz,* 10 Ohio St. 21, 23, 15 N.E. 359, 360 (1890) (dictum). Note, however, that if the dictum appears on the first page of the case in one of the reporters cited, it is unnecessary to repeat this page number in the citation. *Brag v. Snort,* 112 Va. 542, 543, 158 S.E. 615 (1929) (dictum).

(2) Concurring or dissenting opinions. If a dissenting or concurring opinion is cited, indicate that fact in parentheses at the end of the citation. *McLaughlin v. Walter,* 250 Pa. 206, 218, 195 A. 417, 425 (1915) (concurring opinion). To name the judge, cite: *See* Mr. Justice Black, dissenting in *Harkness v. Cass,* 315 U.S. 419, 480 (1939); or *Harkness v. Cass,* 315 U.S. 419, 480 (1939) (Black, J., dissenting).

(3) Points decided by implication; Alternative Holdings. Where the point for which the case is cited is obtained by implication, or where there is an alternative basis of decision, such should be indicated parenthetically. *Shayne v. David,* 21 U.S. (8 Wheat.) 22 (1823) (by implication); *Hobart v. Parson,* 20 Ohio St. 34 (1873) (alternative holding).

(4) Plurality opinions. If an opinion was joined by only a plurality of judges, indicate the fact parenthetically. *Frontiero v. Richardson,* 411 U.S. 677 (1973) (plurality opinion).

(5) Points with holding unclear. If the holding of a case is not clear, indicate this fact by "holding unclear" in parentheses at the end of the citation. *Sacks v. Hart,* 325 U.S. 1 (1945) (holding unclear).

b. Explanatory Parentheticals

(1) Name of judge writing opinion. The name of the judge who wrote the opinion and other information relevant to the weight of the authority cited may be given in parentheses. *Ewing v. Ames,* 115 F.2d 25 (2d Cir. 1952) (L. Hand, J.).

(2) Statement of facts. A brief statement of the facts or a comment on the case which helps explain the citation may also be enclosed in parentheses. *Greeley v. Jones,* 10 Hawaii 16 (1959) (joint tortfeasors); *Begley v. Louis,* 18 Vt. 127 (1864) (common law rule).

c. Order of Parentheticals. Parentheticals indicating weight should precede those giving other information. *Briffaut v. Gelston,* 219 Mass. 14, 191 N.E. 12 (1923) (by implication) (per curiam) ($10,000 verdict not excessive).

D. CITATION OF CASES

1. GENERAL RULES OF FORM

a. Parts of the Citation (Order and Form). Parts of a citation are given in the following order and form:

(1) Case name. Names of both parties and the "v." between them are underlined (the equivalent of italics) and followed by a comma. *Langevoort v. Sidorov,* 422 U.S. 483 (1976). The parties' names can be shortened for the purpose of citation. Rules providing for such shortening are listed in subsections b and c of this part. In citing administrative decisions, use the full name of the first named party.

(2) Reporter. This part of the citation gives (a) the volume number, (b) the name of the reporter, and (c) the page number in the reporter on which the decision begins.

Abbreviations of the names of the reporters to be used may be found below in Parts D.2. and D.3.

If the reporter name is not sufficient to indicate which court made the decision, the court must be indicated in parentheses with the date at the end of the citation. *McDonald v. Cooper,* 254 Misc. 498, 50 N.Y.S.2d 891 (Sup.Ct.1959).

(3) Date. The year is enclosed in parentheses at the end of the citation.

(4) Subsequent and prior history. The prior and subsequent history of a case may be a necessary part of the citation. The subsections below explain when such history is required. The history is explained by underlined explanatory words between the citations.

(a) Subsequent History. The subsequent history of a case is always given whenever the case is cited in full, with the exceptions that the history on remand and any denial of rehearing are omitted unless relevant for that which the case is cited. Note the use of commas. *Abrams v. Cushing,* 101 Mass. 362, 48 N.E. 384 (1901), *aff'd,* 200 U.S. 201 (1904); *Simkowitz v. Wyse,* 120 Pa. 381, 43 N.E. 760 (1911), *cert. denied,* 98 U.S. 859 (1912); *Donald J. Dietrich,* 39 T.C. 271 (1962), *rev'd,* 330 F.2d 985 (6th Cir. 1964).

(b) Prior History. The prior history of a case is given only if significant to the point for which the case is cited.

(c) Use of *"sub nom."* This phrase is used if the names of the parties differ on appeal. It is not used when the names of the parties are simply reversed. *Griswold v. Hall,* 282 F.2d 600 (1st Cir. 1960), *rev'd per curiam sub*

nom.   Toepfer v. Hall, 370 U.S. 400 (1962).   Note that
there is no comma after *"nom."   Sub nom.* is used only
with subsequent, not prior history.

b.   Omissions in Case Names

(1) Secondary parties.   Names of all parties (except the first
listed on each side) and words (such as *et al.*) which indicate
multiple parties are omitted.   However, no portion of a part-
nership name may be omitted.

(2) Procedural phrases.   Ex parte, In re, and other procedural
phrases can be omitted only in administrative actions and
when adversary parties are named.   *Ex rel.,* however, is retained even when adversary parties are named.

(3) Given names and initials.   Those names of individuals are
omitted in all but administrative actions, but names of busi-
ness firms must always be given in full.

(4) State names.   "State of," "Commonwealth of," and "People
of" are omitted except in citing decisions of that state, in which
case only "People", "Commonwealth", or "State" should be
retained.   *Wolf v. Colorado,* 325 U.S. 25 (1949);   *State v. Lehman,* 218 Miss. 412, 96 So. 2d 130 (1957);   not *State of Mississip-
pi v. Lehman.*

(5) Phrases of location.   Phrases of location (such as ". . . of
Boston") are omitted unless this leaves only one word in the
name of a party or corporation or is the designation of a
national or larger geographical area.   Note: "of America" is
always omitted after "United States."

(6) Consolidated actions.   If a case is the consolidation of two
or more actions, cite only the first listed.

c.   Abbreviations in Case Names

(1) Commonly abbreviated full names.   When the entire name
of a party is commonly abbreviated to widely recognized initials, this may be done in the citation.

(2) Abbreviations of words within names.   A word which is
commonly abbreviated may be shortened in a citation if it is
not the first word of the name of a party.   Some words in this
category are: Commissioner (Comm'r); Company (Co.); Consolidated (Consol.); Corporation (Corp.); Department (Dep't);
Electric (Elec.); Insurance (Ins.); Mutual (Mut.); National
(Nat'l); Society (Soc'y).

(3) Railroads.   In giving railroad names, the first word is
generally given in full, and the others abbreviated to the initial
letter unless the name is very short or there is a recognized
abbreviation for it or the words complete the name of a state,
city or geographical entity begun by the first word.   "Co." is

never included. "R.R." or "Ry." is used as the abbreviation of "Railroad Company" or "Railway Company." *Baltimore & O.R.R. v. United States ex rel. Minneapolis, St. P. & Ste. M. Ry.; Lehigh Valley R.R. v. New York Cent. R.R.*

2. CITATIONS TO REPORTERS OF FEDERAL CASES

a. Supreme Court of the United States

(1) If the official report has appeared. Citation to the official United States Reporter is sufficient for Supreme Court cases. *Jones v. Jones,* 206 U.S. 356 (1935). When citing any of the first 90 volumes of this reporter, indicate both the number of the volume as renumbered and the name of the report editor. *Green v. Biddle,* 21 U.S. (8 Wheat.) 16 (1823). Beginning with 91 U.S. (1875) the named reporter is disregarded and cases are cited simply as "U.S." The names of the cited report editors follow in the chronological order of their reports:

Dallas (cited: Dall.) (4 vol.) (1–4 U.S.)

Cranch (cited: Cranch) (9 vol.) (5–13 U.S.)

Wheaton (cited: Wheat.) (12 vol.) (14–25 U.S.)

Peters (cited: Pet.) (16 vol.) (26–41 U.S.)

Howard (cited: How.) (24 vol.) (42–65 U.S.)

Black (cited: Black) (2 vol.) (66–67 U.S.)

Wallace (cited: Wall.) (23 vol.) (68–90 U.S.)

(2) If the official report has not appeared. If the official report has not yet appeared, cite to Supreme Court Reporter (cited: S. Ct.), or, if not therein, to the United States Law Week (cited: U.S.L.W.). In the latter case, indicate the date of the decision, and the court. *Chandler v. Wilson,* 23 U.S.L.W. 406 (U.S. Nov. 8, 1954).

b. Lower Federal Courts

(1) Federal Reporter and Federal Reporter, Second Series (since 1880) (Cited: F. and F.2d). These unofficial reporters have achieved approximately official status through constant use in the absence of an official reporter.

The court from which the decision came must be specially noted in parentheses since F. and F.2d cover a multitude of courts. The following courts are covered:

(a) Courts of Appeals. There are thirteen of these, one for each of the eleven regional circuits, one for the District of Columbia and one for the Federal Circuit. The number of the circuit must be included in the citation. *Jones v. Jones,* 173 F.2d 25 (1st Cir. 1949); *Mills v. Wilber,* 280 F. 25 (D.C. Cir. 1919).

(b) Circuit Courts (abolished 1912). *Cahoon v. Sand,* 180 F. 35 (C.C.S.D.N.Y. 1911).

(c) District Courts. There is at least one district court for each of the 50 states. In citing, name the district but not any division within it. Proper citation for United States District Court for the Eastern District of Illinois, Western Division, would be: *Jones v. Jones,* 180 F. 35 (E.D. Ill. 1901).

(d) Court of Customs and Patent Appeals. This should be cited to the official reporter only in the absence of the federal reporter. *Jones v. Jones,* 98 F.2d 73 (C.C.P.A. 1936).

(e) Court of Claims. This should be cited to the official reporter only in the absence of the federal reporter. *Gardiner v. Lyons,* 98 F.2d 73 (Ct.Cl. 1936).

(2) Federal Supplement (since 1932) (cited: F. Supp.). This includes decisions of the District Courts and of the Court of Claims (see above under Federal Reporter). *Cohen v. Hassett,* 192 F. Supp. 841 (S.D.N.Y. 1965); *Klein v. Gilbert,* 330 F. Supp. 210 (D.R.I. 1970).

(3) Federal Rules Decisions (since 1938) (cited: F.R.D.). This work includes decisions of all federal courts interpreting and applying the Federal Rules of Criminal and Civil Procedure. If the same case is printed in both F.R.D. and F. Supp. or F.2d cite to the latter only. The court must be indicated if the sole cite is to F.R.D.

(4) Federal Cases. Federal Cases contains many of the federal court cases decided prior to 1880. The decisions in the thirty volumes are arranged alphabetically and not chronologically, each case being numbered. Proper citation is: *Jones v. Smith,* 14 F. Cas. 452 (No. 7312) (C.C.S.D.N.J.1870).

(5) The Circuit Court of Appeals Reports (cited: C.C.A.). These are now discontinued and because their materials since 1880 are also included in the Federal Reporter, citation to this special series should not be used unless the case is not reported in the National Reporter System or in Federal Cases.

(6) American Law Reports, Annotated (cited: A.L.R., A.L.R.2d, A.L.R.3d) (1919—to date). American Law Reports contains selected state and federal cases, some of which are extensively annotated.

c. **Administrative Bodies.** Cite only to the official report if the case appears therein. Use only the full name of the first named party in citing reports of administrative bodies. *Ernest J. Brown,* 27 B.T.A. 660 (1932). If the official report has not yet been bound and paginated, cite by case number and full date. *Mario v. Carpaty,* 29 T.C. No. 12 (Dec. 22, 1968).

d. Incomplete Citations

(1) Where there is no official citation. If for any reason a case does not appear or has not yet appeared in the official reports, cite only the unofficial reporter. *Jones v. Jones,* 256 S. Ct. 209 (1969); *Keeton v. O'Connell,* 218 So. 2d 842 (Fla. 1968).

(2) Where the case has not yet appeared in any report. The full texts of United States Supreme Court and other federal court opinions can generally be found very soon after they are rendered in the United States Law Week, which should be cited if it is the only available reference. *Jones v. Mullaney,* 26 U.S.L.W. 4416 (U.S. Jan. 7, 1959). If the opinion does not appear in any report, then the following form may be used: *Jones v. Jones,* Civil No. 51–1250 (D.Mass., filed Mar. 1, 1959).

3. CITATIONS TO REPORTERS OF STATE CASES

State court cases should be cited to both the official reporter and one unofficial reporter. Cases reported with independent pagination in two reports of the National Reporter System (New York Court of Appeals cases since 1 N.Y.2d 1 and California Supreme Court cases since 53 Cal.2d 187) should be cited to the official and both West reporters. *Stimley v. Starzel,* 114 N.H. 84, 176 N.E.2d 155 (1957); *Hassett v. Wood,* 2 N.Y.2d 727, 138 N.E.2d 729, 157 N.Y.S.2d 364 (1956); *Schuldofer v. Dodge,* 60 Cal. 2d 208, 359 P.2d 35, 50 Cal. Rptr. 47 (1960).

a. Official Reporters

(1) Abbreviation of state names. The names of all states and territories (except Alaska, Hawaii, Idaho, Iowa, Ohio and Utah) are abbreviated in citations as follows: Ala., Ariz., Ark., Cal., C.Z., Colo., Conn., Del., D.C., Fla., Ga., Ill., Ind., Kan., Ky., La., Me., Md., Mass., Mich., Minn., Miss., Mo., Mont., Neb., Nev., N.H., N.J., N.M., N.Y., N.C., N.D., Okla., Or., Pa., P.R., R.I., S.C., S.D., Tenn., Tex., Vt., V.I., Va., Wash., W.Va., Wis., Wyo.

(2) Early state reports. The early state reports were prepared by and listed under the names of individual reporters. Proper abbreviations of these early reports may be found in the appendix of *Black's Law Dictionary.* The abbreviations for the more commonly cited early reports appear in *A Uniform System of Citation* (13th ed. 1981). Where the jurisdiction is not shown by such a citation, it should appear in the parentheses with the date. *Jones v. Doe,* 4 Wend. 10 (N.Y. 1835). *Roe v. Smith,* 5 Wend. 13, 12 Am. Dec. 68 (N.Y. 1836).

(3) Exceptional state reports. In most jurisdictions the official reporter covers only the decisions of the highest appellate

court in the state. The court need not be specifically named where this is the case, since the information as to the court is conveyed by the name of the report itself. In other jurisdictions there are several courts reported in a single reporter. In this latter situation, it is always necessary to indicate the particular court from which the decision came unless the court is the highest in the state. If the court is clear from the name of the reporter the court of decision need not be indicated even if it is not the highest in the state. *Morris v. Benbassat,* 210 P.2d 887 (Okla. 1955); *Fried v. Adler,* 28 App. Div. 2d 73, 14 N.Y.S.2d 449 (1951). A list of official state reporters which cover more than one court and official reporters cited other than merely by name of the state alone can be found in *A Uniform System of Citation* (14th ed. 1986).

b. **Unofficial Reporters**

(1) National Reporter System (West). This is the most desirable of all unofficial reporters to cite, but the first of the West series began in 1879. The West Company puts out the regional reporters covering state court cases, with most now appearing in the second series for the region. The proper citation and citation spacing for each sectional reporter is given below.

Reporter	1st Series	2d Series
Atlantic	A.	A.2d
California	Cal. Rptr.	
New York Supplement	N.Y.S.	N.Y.S.2d
North Eastern	N.E.	N.E.2d
North Western	N.W.	N.W.2d
Pacific	P.	P.2d
Southern	So.	So. 2d
South Eastern	S.E.	S.E.2d
South Western	S.W.	S.W.2d

(2) Annotated Reports System. The reporters within this system are as selective as the West System is complete. However, for cases prior to 1879, these will provide an unofficial reporter citation. Since 1888, the major emphasis has been upon printing cases of widespread interest and including an annotation. See the section on citing secondary authority for the form of citing the annotation alone. Citation should include parenthetical indication of court and jurisdiction.

American Law Reports Annotated (A.L.R.; A.L.R.2d; A.L.R.3d)

Lawyers' Reports Annotated (Note: This series had two further series, the second being called "New Series" and the third being called "Dated Series." The following illustrates the correct citation form, with the date of 1915 being illustrative for the "Dated Series": L.R.A.; L.R.A. (n.s.); 1915 L.R.A.).

American Annotated Cases (Am. Ann. Cas.)

American and English Annotated Cases (Am. & Eng.Ann. Cas.)

American State Reports (Am. St. R.)

American Reports (Am. R.)

American Decisions (Am. Dec.)

c. Incomplete Citations

(1) Where there is no official citation. Sometimes a case will appear in an unofficial and not in the official reports, particularly if it is from a lower state court. Cite the unofficial reporter, including the jurisdiction or court in the parentheses before the date. *Jones v. Jones,* 176 N.E. 28 (Ill. 1965). *Jones v. Jones,* 137 N.Y.S. 25 (Sup. Ct. 1925).

(2) Where the case has not yet appeared in any report. Cite by docket number, court and full date. *Black v. White,* Civil No. 51–1250 (Pa. Super. Ct. May 1, 1959).

E. CITATION OF STATUTES AND CONSTITUTIONS

1. IN GENERAL

a. Session Laws and Compilations. Statute reports may roughly be divided into two classes, session laws and compilations. The session laws are usually printed in the chronological order of enactment and are nearly always official reports of the legislature; compilations are usually arranged according to subject matter and may or may not have official status. Because of the large variety of titles which are employed, it is impossible to give a list of both classes for each state and their proper method of citation.

(1) Compilations. Cite a state statute only to the latest official statutory compilation, if it appears therein. The official compilations are not always up to date, and they may not include all of the statutes. In the latter event, cite the statute to the unofficial compilation. Ill. Rev. Stat. ch. 111½, §§ 35.27–.31 (1963); Mass. Gen. Laws Ann. ch. 94, § 19 (1954); Tenn. Code Ann. § 8582 (1955).

(2) Session Laws. If the statute is contained in neither official nor unofficial compilations, cite it to the session laws. 1975 N.Y. Laws.

b.　General Rules on Form.　In contrast to cases, statutes are not underlined or italicized.　Statutes are primary authorities and should be listed as such in the Table of Citations.　A listing of the statutes cited should precede a listing of the secondary authorities used.

2.　FEDERAL STATUTES

a.　General Form of Citation.　In citing United States statutes that are in those parts of the United States Code which have been enacted into positive law, indicate only the title, section and date of the code along with the name of the statute if it has one.　Declaratory Judgment Act, 28 U.S.C. §§ 2201–02 (1959).　The titles of U.S.C. which have been enacted into positive law as of 1982 are titles 1, 3–5, 9–11, 13, 14, 17, 18, 23, 28, 31, 32, 35, 37–39, 44 and 49.

For all other titles the language of United States Statutes at Large (cited: Stat.) is authoritative.　Both United States Code and United States Code Annotated (cited: U.S.C.A.) cross-reference code sections to U.S. Statutes at Large.　U.S. Statutes at Large need not be cited unless the language in the U.S. Statutes at Large differs materially from that in United States Code.　Clayton Act, 15 U.S.C. § 16 (1959);　Federal Trade Commission Act, 38 Stat. 747 (1914), 15 U.S.C. § 78 (1959).

b.　Amended Statutes.　It may be relevant that the statutory language being cited differs from an earlier or later version of the statute.　The following rules indicate how this information, if desired, may be conveyed in the citation.

(1) When a section is amended so that the subsequent version completely supersedes and repeals the earlier version, the version now in force is cited to the code and the version no longer in force is cited to the session laws.　If discussing the former version, cite: Clayton Act sec. 7, ch. 25, sec. 7, 38 Stat. 730 (1914), *amended by* 15 U.S.C. sec. 18 (1964).　If discussing the present version, cite: Clayton Act sec. 7, 15 U.S.C. § 18 (1964), *formerly* ch. 25, sec. 7, 38 Stat. 730 (1914).

(2) When a statutory section is amended so that the subsequent version only makes additions to and does not repeal the former, cite both versions to the code.　In discussing the present version, cite: 28 U.S.C. § 2201(b) (Supp. I 1965), *amending* 28 U.S.C. § 2201 (1964).　If discussing the former version, cite: 28 U.S.C. § 2201 (1964), *as amended,* 28 U.S.C. § 2201(b) (Supp. I 1965).

c.　New Statutes.　Statutes enacted since the last complete United States Code should be cited by the most recent U.S.C. Supplement.　United States Mandamus Act, 28 U.S.C. § 83 (Supp. V 1964).

Statutes enacted subsequent to the last U.S.C. Supplement should be cited by U.S.C.A. pocket supplements. 18 U.S.C.A. § 14 (Supp.1965).

d. Statutes No Longer in Force and Statutes Not Appearing in Any Edition of United States Code. These are cited by reference only to the Statutes at Large (cited: Stat.). Give the chapter number and the name or the full date if there is no name. The fact that the act is no longer in force as cited must be indicated parenthetically. Act of Sept. 8, 1950, ch. 924, § 2, 64 Stat. 798 (repealed 1955). Since the 85th Congress, the public law number should be used in place of the chapter number.

e. Statutes Enacted by the Current Legislature. These are cited: Pub. L. No. 94–32, § 20(a) (June 11, 1975). "94–" means "94th Congress."

f. Internal Revenue Code. When dealing with federal tax questions, cite the Internal Revenue Code of 1954, if the section cited is in force at the time of writing. I.R.C. § 301 (1984). Sections of the Internal Revenue Code of 1939 must be cited to Int. Rev. Code of 1939, ch. 1, § 115(d), 53 Stat. 47 (now I.R.C. § 301). Revenue Acts prior to 1939 are cited by name and to Stat. Revenue Act of 1924, ch. 234, § 200, 43 Stat. 454.

g. Rules of Procedure. The Federal Rules of Civil and Criminal Procedure may conveniently be cited as statutes. Fed. R. Civ. P. 19(b); Fed. R. Crim. P. 42(b).

3. STATE STATUTES

a. Official Compilation. Cite state statutes to the latest official compilation; if not contained there, cite the statute to the preferred unofficial compilation. Ill. Rev. Stat. ch. 32, § 439.50 (1963); Mass. Gen. Laws ch. 41, § 95 (1932); N.J. Rev. Stat. § 43:22–5 (Supp. 1955).

b. Unofficial Compilation. If the statute has been amended or enacted subsequent to the most recent supplement to the official compilation, cite the preferred unofficial compilation. Pa. Stat. Ann. tit. 2, § 4656.13 (1959).

c. New York and California Codes. The New York and California Codes are cited by the name of the particular law or code with indication of date and edition. Cal. Agric. Code § 351 (West 1954); N.Y. Banking Law § 121 (McKinney 1964).

d. Uniform Acts. Uniform acts cited as the law of a particular state should be cited to the state statute in the manner described above. When citing a uniform act as such (that is, when not citing it as the law of any particular state), there is no requirement that the date of promulgation be given, unless the act has been withdrawn. Uniform Warehouse Receipts Act § 40 (withdrawn 1906). The Uniform Commercial Code is cited in abbreviated form. U.C.C. § 2–505.

4. ENGLISH STATUTES

Cite the name, year of sovereign's reign, chapter, and section.

Statute of Gloucester, 1278, 6 Edw. 1, c. 8, § 1; Copyright Act, 1911, 1 & 2 Geo. V, c. 46, § 2. Where the statute has no name or where the name does not include the date, put the date in parentheses at the end. After 1962, regnal years are omitted.

5. CONSTITUTIONS

Constitutions should precede statutes in any listing (for instance, in the Table of Citations section of the brief), but are cited under the general heading of statutes. U.S. Const. art. III, § 8; U.S. Const. amend. XIV, § 2; Mont. Const. art. 8, § 16.

The date is given only where a constitution other than the one in force is cited. Ga. Const. art. II, § 1 (1875).

F. CITATION TO SECONDARY AUTHORITY

1. AMERICAN LAW INSTITUTE RESTATEMENTS

Publications of the American Law Institute should be cited as follows:

Restatement of Torts § 90 (1936).

Restatement (Second) of Conflict of Laws § 20 (1958).

Restatement of Trusts § 9, comment *b* (1935).

Restatement of Contracts § 106 (Tent. Draft No. 1, 1929).

Restatement of Agency Neb. Annot. § 5 (1934).

7 *A.L.I. Proceedings* 256 (1930).

2. TREATISES

Citations to treatises should follow these rules.

a. Name of author. The name is cited with the last name and first initial, unless more would aid identification. W. Prosser.

b. Title of book (underlined or italicized).

c. Page or section number.

d. Edition and year (in parentheses).

e. The volume number of a multiple volume work precedes the name of the author. The following are examples of single and multiple volume works: R. Brooks & W. Warren, *Understanding Poetry* 524 (1938); 2 F. Wharton, *Criminal Law and Procedure* § 572 (12th ed. 1957).

f. There is no comma between the title and the section or page number.

g. The page or section number may be omitted in the Table of Citations, particularly if many sections are cited.

h. Always cite to the most recent edition of a work which gives the matter in question. 1 S. Williston, *Sales* § 72 (rev. ed. 1948).

i. In special cases treatises are identified by the editor: 5 *American Law of Property* § 22.15 (A.J. Casner ed. 1952).

j. In a few time-honored works the edition is left out and the star page, the page of the original printing, is referred to. 2 W. Blackstone, *Commentaries* * 152. E. Coke, *Littleton* * 5.

3. LAW REVIEW ARTICLES AND NOTES

Abbreviations of the names of law reviews are listed in *A Uniform System of Citation* (13th ed. 1981). Note that California is abbreviated to Calif.; Columbia, to Colum.; and that Texas is not abbreviated.

a. Leading Articles. Citations of leading articles should give the following information in the following order:

(1) Author (last name and first initial), followed by a comma.

(2) Title of article (underlined), followed by a comma.

(3) Volume of law review. If the periodical has no volume number, use the year of publication. 67 Harv. L. Rev. 710 (1955); 1938 Wis. L. Rev. 307.

(4) Name of review.

(5) Page number on which article begins. Exception: if the article appears in two or more parts, cite the page number upon which each part begins. But when citing to specific material within one part, give only the first page of that part and the page upon which the material appears. Fuller, *Legal Fictions,* 25 Ill. L. Rev. 363, 513, 865 (1930–31).

(6) Date (in parentheses).

b. Law Review Notes and Comments. Student material, other than short commentaries, is cited by the designation used in the publishing review. The name of a student author is never given, but the title is always included. Note, *Speluncean Explorers,* 45 Colum. L. Rev. 382 (1945); Comment, *Civil Rights Act,* 49 Mich. L. Rev. 261 (1950).

Short commentaries, such as Recent Decisions and Case Notes, are cited without identification. 8 U. Chi. L. Rev. 132 (1940).

Recent case write-ups are cited: 28 Colum. L. Rev. 130 (1928). When these are used together with the case, cite: *Beale v. Williston,* 71 F.2d 334 (2d Cir. 1934), *noted in* 43 Yale L.J. 881. If the date of the write-up differs, give both dates: *Jones v. York,* 310 Mass. 613, 8 N.E.2d 790 (1939), *noted in* 53 Harv. L. Rev. 806 (1940).

4. ANNOTATIONS

As a general rule, do not cite decisions to the A.L.R. or L.R.A. These materials may, however, be used for an additional unofficial citation where the cited case is reported therein and is the subject of an annotation. Indicate the page upon which the report, not the annotation, begins. When citing the annotation alone, indicate the page upon which the annotation begins, and the date of publication of the volume. Annot., 12 A.L.R.2d 382 (1950).

5. ADDITIONAL SOURCES

a. Encyclopedias. On very rare occasions, additional sources might include references to Corpus Juris, Corpus Juris Secundum, American Jurisprudence, American Jurisprudence 2d, and Ruling Case Law. These, in the order just given, are cited for the subject heading "Trial" as follows: 29 C.J. *Trial* § 24 (1944); 33 C.J.S. *Trial* § 21 (1955); 19 Am.Jur. *Trial* § 21 (1946); 6 Am.Jur.2d *Assignments* § 7 (1957); 19 R.C.L. *Trial* § 21 (1952).

b. Newspapers. In citing newspapers give the name of the paper, the full date, the section (if any), the page, and the column. N.Y. Times, Jan. 21, 1936, § 3, at 1, col. 4. A signed article (but not a news report) is cited by author and title.

c. Briefs. Citation of an opponent's brief or an earlier brief (*e.g.,* citation of appellant's brief in his own reply brief) in the same litigation need only identify the brief and page. Brief for Appellee at 10. If a brief in another lawsuit is cited, the case must be clearly identified. Brief for Appellant at 26, *Burka v. Cogan,* 248 F.2d 60 (D.C.Cir. 1974).

INDEX

References are to Pages

†